Imposter

An Autobiography

Jim Whelan

Contents

Published in 2021 by
AG Books
www.agbooks.co.uk

Acknowledgements

There are so many people to thank for my book. I sent it, more in hope than anything else, to the lovely Sara Cox to be edited. She told me that it was worth trying to publish; here is the result. Elizabeth at Narrow Road has been my agent for nearly twenty years, I am so grateful to be looked after so well. Joe Larkins at AG Books has been a fount of knowledge, I am so lucky to have found him. My luck was meeting Harry Pope, who introduced me, thanks Harry. Tony Flood has been an encouraging presence for which I am so grateful. John Lauper just helps me, all the time, never looking for anything but thanks. The Grandboys, Ben, Lucas and Thomas for whom this is written, in the hope that they may read this one day to show them how life used to be. My mate, my son Andrew, and my lovely, so caring daughter Lucy. Most of all my Helen. Someone was looking out for me when you came into my life, thank you for putting up with me all these years darling.

I would like to dedicate this book to my lovely Helen.
She has been my rock for so many years, without her I am nothing.

Why Imposter?

I have never walked onto a TV or Film set or arrived at a Theatre for the first day of rehearsal without feeling the dread that someone will tap me on the shoulder and say, "Hey, you're not an actor, go away".

For a shy, insecure child, to a teenager with no sense of worth, putting myself up in front of everybody to be scrutinised and perhaps ridiculed would seem impossible, and yet I feel the greatest joy from it all. I love the rehearsals, the read-throughs, the companionship and the sure knowledge that we all feel the same to some degree.

So, I have followed my dream, had extraordinary times along the way, worked with people who are a hundred times more talented than me, fallen in love, helped to bring up our children and felt the great joy of grandchildren.

Heading for my ninth decade, I want to chronicle some highs and lows. Here they are.

Imposter

1: Vera's Funeral

"I want complete and utter silence on set," John Folkard, the floor manager said, to some of the most famous actors in the land.

We were preparing to shoot the pivotal scene at Vera Duckworth's funeral, and Jack was about to pay tribute to his beloved 'swamp duck'.

I had first met Bill some 40 years earlier, one miserable Friday night when we were both club entertainers and worked at Tonge Ward Labour Club in Bolton. He had a fine singing voice back then.

In between scenes, Bill Tarmey asked me to come outside to have a chat while he smoked another fag. His fingers were nicotine stained, and his voice rasped when he said, "I've told them I'm leaving the Street this year It's getting too much."

I can't say it came as a complete surprise because he didn't look well; he'd had heart trouble for many years and couldn't stop smoking. As a result, his breathing was laboured, and his chest rattled whenever he spoke.

I was playing my usual part as the Reverend Todd, officiating at Vera's committal and my role was to say a few words and then ask if anyone wanted to speak.

As usual, my mouth was dry and my hands were trembling as the scene approached, you might think that it would be easy after so many years; it was not. We were in the tiny Crematorium Chapel in Southern Cemetery in Manchester and crammed into the pews looking on at Bill and I, was practically the complete *Coronation Street* cast. It flitted through my brain that this scene would eventually be watched by up to 12 million people. I tried to put it out of my mind.

My first appearance in 'The Street' had been in 1965 and so much had happened to me since then.

I tried to forget everything else and concentrated fiercely on the scene.

"Action" said John.

After a few homilies, I said to the congregation. "Vera was a very special lady. Would anyone like to say a few words?"

There was an awkward silence, and then Jack Duckworth spoke. "Yes vicar, I'd like to say something." He shuffled a bit awkwardly to the lectern and pulled a piece of paper from his inside pocket, trying to smooth it on the polished wood.

Sniffles were heard from the congregation as Jack spoke simply and humbly about his first meeting with his 'Vee', how they had squabbled affectionately for many years and how he was missing her. The tears from the likes of Tyrone, Deirdre, Rita and Emily were not all the result of acting; many were genuine. This was the end of an era in *Coronation Street*.

Liz Dawn's characterisation of Vera Duckworth had made her a much-loved person, and although we knew that it was not real, nonetheless the emotion of saying goodbye to her as a work colleague affected lots of the 'regulars'.

I looked around the church, remembering my first meeting with so many of the senior Corrie actors. Barbara Knox, who played Rita Sullivan and I had met at Oldham Rep in 1972 when we did a show together. Ann Kirkbride whose dad was a famous cartoonist used to come into the bar at that time; she was a delightful, pretty, effervescent teenager and was trying to become an actress. Roy Barraclough, who's portrayal of the seedy Alec Gilroy became a highlight of Coronation Street, was also an actor in the Oldham Company. He played Dame in a couple of Pantos which I was in, and as well as being funny, brought a sense of irreverent comedy to the role. I learned so much from my involvement with him, and he remained a good friend. So did Peter Dudley who went on to play Bert Tilsley; he sadly died much too young.

The tears pricked my eyes, and I was glad that I had no more dialogue when Bill finished his eulogy.

How had I, a scruffy war baby from the poorer part of Salford finished up as a recurring character in arguably the best-known programme in the history of British television?

Why had I continued to follow my dream throughout my life, despite my apparent lack of self-confidence, and at the same time, falling in love, getting married, and bringing up a family?

I have been an actor for 50 years. Drama school was never an option for me, and every time I landed a television job, I suffered from the nagging doubt that someone would tap me on the shoulder and say, "hey you, you're not an actor, get off the set."

I have worked with terrific stars like Ray Winstone, David Morrissey, Jeremy Brett, Martin Clunes, David Tennant, Robert Carlisle, Christian Bale, Rod Steiger and Rob Lowe.

I have been directed by such luminaries as Michael Apted, and Todd Haynes and have appeared in some of the most iconic programmes in the history of British television such as *The Royle Family*.

I had to pinch myself sometimes when I found myself alongside such stars as the brilliant Caroline Aherne, and although my status had rarely been higher than that of a 'character actor', no one can take away the memories of being involved with so many talented people over the years.

"OK everybody, that's a wrap thank you very much indeed," said John, and a spontaneous round of applause rang out.

Although the shoot had only taken three days, I was always sad to finish because I had no contract and might never be used again. As we were taken back to the studio in limousines, the usual depression that I always felt when the adrenaline wore off kicked in. I knew that this would not last long, and my mind drifted back to my childhood.

1942 was the year of my birth. Where had the years gone?

2: War Baby

"Right, free dinners over here". We took our places in the queue and waited for fish with yellowing sauce, mashed potatoes and peas. The smell from the stainless steel containers in the serving hatch told us what we were having, so there was no rush.

Nobody thought anything about the fact that there were more kids in the free dinners' line than paying because in Salford just after the Second World War, everyone was poor. Our school dinners were eaten in a hall across the road from the school. They were delivered from a central kitchen about a mile away and were often late. We sat on wooden forms at trestle tables, there was usually a cheer when the *dinner van* – a green Commer commercial, with a Salford City coat of arms on the side – arrived. Then we lined up and they were doled out. There was always mashed spuds and gravy, but the horror as far as I was concerned was the fish on a Friday, which came with 'white' sauce. I could eat almost anything, but this defeated me. Being a good Catholic boy meant that no meat on a Friday was the norm, we did not question it, but I was left with a deep loathing of fish, which continued for many years.

I used to wet the bed, bad enough for a sensitive child, but a hundred times worse was the fact that – knowing no better, and mam not realising – I would go to school wearing the same vest that I had peed on in the night. I started school aged just four, mam took me on the first day, and from then on, I trailed along behind my brother. We got up on our own, had a jam butty, and crossed two busy main roads with no crossing persons. As the radiators heated up the classroom, I would reek of wee, and the other kids would call me 'smelly Whelan'. I had a fight nearly every day because of this. I was convinced that I was inferior, and I could never rid myself of the feeling that deep down inside, I was rotten. It hurts me even now to admit that the sleeves of my jumper were silver with snot because I wiped my nose on them all the time.

My brother Christopher started school a year before me. He was the oldest. I was next, my sister Eileen was two years younger than me, Philip was born on VJ day in 1945, and the youngest, Billy, came along in 1946. It hardly needs saying that five kids in seven years put a strain on the family finances.

Saint Thomas of Canterbury Catholic primary School did its utmost to indoctrinate us, we jumped to attention when Dean Daly, our parish priest, came into the classroom and we recited the Catechism to the best of our ability. My first teacher was Miss Brown, she was a kindly soul and did her best to instil some kind of discipline into a class of thirty-six, mostly scruffy kids, but with nearly all of us she was wasting her time, we were cannon fodder, and destined for labouring jobs. The schoolwork was never very demanding for me. I was mostly invisible apart from my fighting, but this was the way I wanted it.

In our class there were three boys who might pass the Holy Grail of the 11 plus when we were ten, but I was not one of them and just jogged gently along in the middle of the pack. As the second of five children in our first-generation Irish family, there was no reason for anyone to think that I was anything out of the ordinary, and indeed any brains I might have had were kept well hidden.

Higher Broughton, Salford was a very mixed district. Just up the road from our house was Broughton Park, quite an affluent Jewish area. When we were young, we used to 'scrump' apples from the gardens of the big houses. On a couple of occasions, we were caught and told, that if we knocked on the door, we could have all the apples we wanted. It had never occurred to us.

My very first memories were of the cold. I have since heard that 1947 was a terrible winter, and I recall crying because I didn't want to get out of bed onto a freezing cold floor. One thing my older brother and I had to do every morning was light the fire. We first had to go down into the cellar, chop up some wood for kindling, and empty the grate. Even from a distance of seventy-five years, I can remember going down into the cellar, picking up the heavy axe, and trying to split an old plank from a bombed-out house. The misery of the cold, and the dark dampness use to frighten me, but there was no way out. Lighting the thing was always difficult for me – I was too young – but if the wood didn't light, I would put a shovel up to the fireplace, and then newspaper to cover the grate to cause a draft. If all else failed, I would throw a handful of sugar on it. I still don't understand why, but it used to make it flare up. I asked Chris some years back if we really did that, or had I mis-remembered, because I was a little four-year-old. He said that his memories were the same.

We lived in a large draughty Victorian semi on a main road. I never remember anything being done to the house in the way of repairs, or to the garden, which was overgrown with weeds. I have a distinct memory of army tanks driving up the main road each morning, and me and my brother Chris sitting on the garden wall waving. Over the road was a patch of waste ground which had been bombed and this site, which we called the 'croft', was our playground when we were growing up. We had to be careful every morning to empty out our boots or wellies before putting them on, as we were plagued with beetles, which we called Blackjacks, and they used to like to lie in wait in our footwear. The house had gaunt giant attics, which we would play in when the weather was bad; we could see the roofs and smokestack of Strangeways prison, and just behind it, the big sooty buildings of Manchester City Centre, known to everyone locally as 'Town'.

I have some happy memories of being read to by my mam, but as there were others to be looked after, I soon became quite solitary. I could not rid myself of the shame of my bed-wetting. My self-esteem was never high, and I mostly retreated into my shell.

My mam Sara always seemed to be working when we were small. She would go to her first cleaning job for four hours in the morning, do her second cleaning job in the afternoon, come home and feed us all, clean up our mess and sit down to sew buttons on trousers for the Jewish tailor who lived next door, sometimes until the early hours. There were fourteen buttons on each pair, and it would take her half an hour to sew them on. For each pair she finished she would receive one shilling and sixpence. We kids thought nothing of this, we took it as the norm that mam would be always on the go.

Mother was from the west of Ireland, county Mayo. She had come over to England before the war, to escape the extreme poverty, met my Dad, who was from Dublin, and married. I never met my maternal grandmother or granddad – I'm not sure they ever left Ireland – but one day when I came home from the Saturday matinee, my mum was crying as she peeled potatoes over the sink in the scullery. When I asked her what the matter was, she simply said, "me dad's dead," and that was that.

My dad was one of eleven children from a Dublin family. Christopher, my brother, and I went to Dublin once and met the extended family but had no contact with them as we were growing up.

The family next door to us were Harry and Millie Alvarez. They had two children, Ann, who was six months older than me, and Michael, the same age as Billy, my youngest brother. My Mum Sara and 'Auntie' Millie became such good friends that they knocked a hole in the wall, which separated our back yards, and would stand gossiping for hours on their own back doorsteps. My mum was never without a Woodbine. It has always seemed to me that

Jewish and Irish people get on well. Because Mum was from the west of Ireland, she made no bones about the fact that she was from a very deprived, impoverished background. How she connected with Millie, who compared to us was middle class, always amazed me, but connect they did.

Ann, Millie's daughter was much more grown up and mature than any of us Whelan kids. I will always be grateful for something that happened when we were about seven. She cornered me in the back yard and said "Jim, why are you always so quiet and miserable?"

I said, "Because nobody likes me."

"Rubbish! We all think you are all right, we just wish you'd play with us a bit more instead of going off on your own." This sounds so wet, but even from the distance of 70 years, I still remember a kind word from a fellow kid. The bed-wetting had stopped some time before, so that was not a problem, but how can a person be so insecure?

Mam was a good violin player and, together with her brother, my uncle Jim – who could get a tune out of anything; accordion, flute, or penny whistle – she would charm us all by having an impromptu concert on St. Patrick's Day. She never drank, but when the chairs were pulled out of the way, she was a wonderful Irish dancer.

There was never enough money and it wasn't until I was older that I realised that this was mainly due to the fact that my dad was not at all fond of work but was deeply in thrall to horseracing. In those days' bookmakers were illegal, but still we would be sent to the ginnel where a little hatch in a back door was opened and we would pass the money through. Needless to say, if there were any winnings my dad collected them for himself.

There was no hiding the fact that my mum and dad did not get on. I can hardly remember a tender word passing between them. Mum was out working, and it was obvious that she was very resentful of my Dad's feckless ways. He often threatened to leave, but never got around to it. He had a bad chest, a legacy of smoking 40 Players a day, and if he got up in a bad mood, we would do our best to keep out of his way. I have to say that he did not physically mistreat us, but a word was enough to strike fear, and we didn't misbehave. If anything as we grew up, Mam and Dad grew even further apart and although they shared the same house, they seldom spoke. For years I thought that this was the way all married couples behaved, and I determined it was not for me, this married life. I came to realise that the typical Irish husband would not be seen dead doing anything around the house, cleaning, cooking, housework, or caring for the children. Certainly, my dad never even washed a cup, whether he was working or not.

3: Shabbos Goy

One of my first jobs as a child was to light fires in the homes of Jewish people in our neighbourhood on Saturdays. The fires were always set; there was no chopping wood, or taking out ashes. I would go to the house in the morning and light the fire, go back at lunchtime to top up with coal, and finally in the evening when I collected my two bob. This gave me the chance to see what to my mind was unimaginable luxury. I found out many years later when I was chatting to a Rabbi in my taxi that I was known as a 'Shabbos goy' and, until central heating became the norm and timers would allow boilers to be pre-programmed, I performed a necessary service.

My inferiority complex stemmed from the free dinners and I think, from experiences like these. Because there was never any money in the house, we wore pumps in the summer, wellies in the winter and scruffy clothes all the time. Living on jam butties was the norm when our mam was out working. I was an over sensitive child and still am quite diffident in certain circumstances. How to square this with continuously trying to put myself on display is something I still struggle with. Perhaps the fact that when I am trying to play a part, I am trying to be someone else helps, or maybe I am an exhibitionist deep down?

When I was made redundant from my 'Shabbos' job, I started doing a paper round. I was 11 years old when I started, even though someone said that I was not supposed to work until the age of 13. This was the worst job I can remember. Having to rise at 6.30am in the cold months was purgatory for me, still the ten shillings a week was useful to mam.

On my round, in amongst the posh houses was the Judges Residence. The circuit Judges would 'lodge' there when sitting at Manchester Assize Courts. I used to hate it when they were in residence, because they would have all the big papers, Times, Guardian, Telegraph etc, and they used to weigh a ton.

My dad would drive me to distraction these mornings. He would get out of bed at 8.30 am and tell me to go and get him a paper, which would make me late for school and I would often get the cane. If I asked him the night before if he wanted a paper in the morning, he shouted that he didn't know, but he was always there in the mornings. I was so angry and frustrated with him. It just wasn't fair.

A memory from those days that is etched on my mind, is delivering to an old soldiers' home on my round. One of the patients had no arms or legs. I used to prop his Daily Express on a rolled-up blanket and open another page for him before I left. I thought nothing of it as a twelve-year-old. It was called Broughton House and is still there, in fact, I used to think that it was rather posh, how little I knew. The War was just something, which had happened, it seemed to be part of nearly every grown up's conversation.

On the morning of my 11 plus examination, I remember thinking that if I passed, I could stop delivering papers and so I decided to give it a real go. I went and sat in church before the exam, said a little prayer, and took it very lightly. Of course, it sounds criminally casual to think like that, but nobody expected anything of me, so I had nothing to lose. The paper did not seem that difficult actually and although I had not been one of the children picked out for special tuition, I thought I acquitted myself well enough, and promptly forgot about it.

When a friend told me one day that he was going to give up his job delivering groceries for John O'Connor and Sons, I screwed up my courage, and went straight to the shop and asked for his job. The manager was a bit surprised as he did not know the other boy was leaving, but as they were now without a delivery boy, he showed me the bike with a cast iron basket in front and off I went. The upside of this was that I now did not have to get up in the mornings, but it was not an easy option because I had to work all day on Saturdays and carry plenty of heavy boxes. An unexpected bonus from those days was that I soon discovered if I was careful, I could help myself to biscuits. They weren't pre-packed then, and they were weighed out into brown paper bags. By being careful, I could untwist the top of the paper bags and gently remove a couple. I became very attached to custard creams.

There is no doubt that I was exploited, but I just did not know it. On Saturdays especially, in between deliveries, I had to weigh out sugar into half pound, pound, and two-pound bags, and butter from a giant slab into greaseproof paper of various sizes. I also learned how to use the cheese wire to cut wedges from the giant slabs that came to us. One of the assistants was an expert at boning the sides of bacon, and he let me watch him, but warned me never, ever to touch the boning knives, which were wickedly sharp. When

I became a little more streetwise, I used to stay out after my deliveries. Still the staff and the manager were kind, and I was reasonably content for more than two years.

I was terribly embarrassed when the manager called me to one side one day and told me to ask my mother to please do something about her 'tick', as she owed nearly ten pounds. I had no idea that we owed money and told my mum in no uncertain terms that this was unacceptable. What a prick! Looking back even from this distance, my poor mum was doing her best with five kids, and no wages coming in from her husband. All she needed was a little dickhead like me to be condescending and look down on her.

4: De La Salle

A couple of months after my 11 plus, a heavy envelope dropped through our door and my mum got deliriously excited as I had passed my 11 plus, one of four from St Thomas'. This was also a worry as I would need a uniform, but she somehow got the money together and I started the next academic year as a pupil of De La Salle College Salford. The teachers at St Thomas' were in a state of shock, I was a dark horse, and they had a hard time believing that there was no mistake.

It would be lovely to report that this was the start of my upward trajectory, but in fact I soon found myself well out of my depth. Academically I would have survived as I was never bottom of my form, but the sheer difference in social class and economics made my life a misery. I was soon singled out as a scruffy sod with a uniform that had hardly changed during all the time I was there. Having to keep doing my job as a delivery boy after school and on Saturdays left me no time for homework or study. My years at De La Salle were the unhappiest of my entire life. Never would I experience such abject misery. I tried first to physically fight my way through as I had done at primary school, but these kids were a different breed. I picked on the class bully, thinking that if I gave a good account of myself, the rest might leave me alone. He was a year above me, and the other boys told me not to take him on, but I thought that I could look after myself. On the playing field after school, he administered a clinical beating that left me physically and mentally demoralised. I knew from then on not to challenge too many of the rugby team. I was to leave at the first opportunity, aged 15, to start work on Salford Docks.

Just before I left school, we had a visit from the dental hygienist. I had never been to a dentist, and I didn't know what to expect. She examined us all, and when she came to me, she said, "you have beautiful teeth young man, but they are green, how often do you clean them?" I had to admit that I had never cleaned them. I had reached the age of fifteen, and had never, ever brushed my teeth. Writing these words over sixty years later, I still feel the shame and embarrassment of that moment. I also had a permanent 'tidemark' round my neck, a further sign that I was not far removed from the 'bog trotting country bumpkin' mentality which my mother imagined that she had left behind. I cried myself to sleep night after night, keeping my distress to myself. My mam was so proud of me, there was no way I could let her down.

Close to my home was North Salford Youth Club and as soon as I was old enough, I joined. It was somewhere to play snooker and table tennis, darts and badminton. It was also somewhere to meet girls, not to speak to, but to look at and blush furiously if they glanced in my direction. Something else that happened there that was to colour my life. The warden was a frightening, abrasive and cantankerous man by the name of Jack Harrison. He ruled with a rod of iron and brooked no argument about anything. One evening he said to me: "Whelan I want you to be in a play for the one act competition, my office 8 o'clock."

When I turned up at his office, there were a further five kids, my heart did a summersault when I saw that three of them were girls.

Jack's office was a sort of inner sanctum where he called people in to discipline them if he found them defacing any of the equipment or giving cheek to any of his assistants. To be fair, this happened rarely because the youth club was well run, the subs were only pennies per week, and we got to listen to the latest records for the last hour, when between 9.00 and 10.00pm, there was dancing.

The dancing always followed the same format, three jives and the one 'smooch', until 9.45pm, when there would be three smooches on the trot, with the lights turned down low. I couldn't jive, and used to wait for the last slow dances, and if I was successful, might get to walk some lucky girl home. If you did get this privilege, the reward would be at most a kiss or two on the doorstep, girls were an unfathomable mystery, they smelled nice, and had funny bumps in different places. They were soft and cuddly, and there was something about them that turned my face a bright red if I thought that they might know what I was thinking. Meeting girls soon cured my tidemark and teeth cleaning deficiencies. I was never out of the bathroom at home. Why had it taken me so long to learn personal hygiene and cleanliness? I even started using underarm roll-on deodorants and 'Old Spice'.

The club opened at seven, and for the first two hours, there was a background of show tune music, such as *South pacific, Carousel, Oklahoma*, and *The King and I*. All of us young members derided these, but I think that by a process of osmosis, having been perhaps not so subtly brainwashed by two hours a night of these, we ended up knowing the songs and tunes, and now I look upon them as part of my teenage years. Although there were plenty of tough kids around in 1950s' Salford, no one wanted to be excluded from the club and behaviour inside was generally good. Many a time, arguments would start inside, but the lads would go outside to fight.

We started to read the play and Jack let us get about four pages through when he slammed his book on his desk and shouted, "that is terrible, I will show you how I want you to do it, every line and you will follow my instructions." We were all nonplussed, but such was the force of his personality that we didn't dare argue and just continued to try to do what he wanted. After an hour or so of this he dismissed us, told us to learn our lines and said that he would see us again in a couple of days. I went home in a kind of a funk, but also felt something exciting was happening and I couldn't sleep. I realised a lot later that this was adrenaline. This feeling has never left me and maybe this is one of the reasons why I have not given up on acting.

The six of us carried on rehearsing with Jack for about three months, twice a week until we were word perfect and would just move or speak within the framework of his vision for the play. When we came to the festival, we won it by a country mile and carried off the cup. Never having been to the theatre, I was amazed that the other groups of youngsters in the competition seemed to be having fun and just enjoying their rehearsals.

As I got to know Jack Harrison a little better and shared a few pints with him, I realised that he had a deep and abiding love of the theatre and decided that the only way he could give his motley under privileged crew a chance in the drama festival was to take them in hand and choreograph their every move and voice inflection. Without even knowing what we were doing, we had for that 35 minutes become the best drama group in the district and the fact that we were robots never occurred to us. Of course, as the years have gone on, I know that this is not the way to get the best out of people and perhaps it wouldn't work anyway with people who were more assertive, nevertheless it gave us a feeling of respect for ourselves. Whether this was what started my obsession with drama I suppose I will never know, but the feeling of terror while waiting to go on stage in a draughty school hall, the buzz of actually losing oneself in a character, and the elation of taking a bow gave me something which even now sticks in my memory.

My unhappy years at De La Salle Grammar were ending. It was made clear to me that neither the head or anyone else would be terribly upset if I left when I reached 15, although 99% stayed until 16, and a high percentage went on to university. My dad said in no uncertain terms that I was to get to work at the earliest opportunity; university was not for the likes of me.

I would certainly not miss the 'Christian Brothers' who ruled us with a rod of iron. The fact that my homework was often late and poorly presented did me no favours. When I got home from school, I had to go out on my bike with the cast iron tray welded onto the front and deliver orders for a couple of hours. I would not get home until 6.30pm, and then if I wanted any peace and quiet, I would have to go upstairs to a freezing bedroom. Consequently, my stuff was rushed and ill thought out and there was no one to turn to at home for help. Many times, I waited trembling outside brother Colombo's study for retribution. Although I was often caned, I cannot say I was particularly badly treated. I do not blame the teachers. I think they just gave up on me but this did nothing to boost my already non-existent self-esteem.

5: The Docks

City of Salford' was emblazoned on all the green buses and public vehicles of the time. Salford was proud of the fact that it was a city and had been granted its charter before Manchester. It had a cathedral on Chapel Street, and a grand market, and cattle market on Cross Lane, leading down to the docks. The docks were always referred to as Salford docks by Salford people. Hanky Park had been immortalised by Walter Greenwood in *Love on the Dole*, and the film *Hobson's choice* with John Mills as Willie Mossop, and Charles Laughton as Hobson, had caused a great stir when shown locally. A few years later Shelagh Delaney made herself famous by writing, *A Taste of Honey*. Looking back, none of these showed us in a great light, but we were not bothered, we knew nowt else.

The tramlines were still in evidence, and I have real memories of riding trams. It used to fascinate me to watch at the terminus when a man would come out with a long pole and change the 'struts' which came out of the top of the carriages, and place them onto a different electrical cable which ran for miles above the main roads. We had to be careful on our bikes not to get the front wheel stuck in the tramlines.

Salford suffered then, and still does from never having a proper town centre. Because we were adjoining Manchester, all the big shops were there, and so there was never a 'Marks & Spencer', or 'H Samuel', and everyone used to head for Market Street, or St Ann's Square. This bred a sort of chip on the shoulder, and Salford always had an inferiority complex about Manchester, and still does to this day.

Growing up there may have been hard but if so, we were never aware of it. We just got on with the usual kids' games and would play out until dark in the summer, playing football for hours on the streets. We never had to worry about money because no one had any. We took the winter smog in our stride. We were used to them and during some of the worst ones, we would try to guide the cars up the road.

The practice when we started work was to hand over the wage packet unopened to our mam, and she would supply us with pocket money, bus fares and dinner money.

My mother would cook a different tea for each member of the family as they came in from work. She wasn't a good cook. She had a giant iron frying pan, and everything went into it; typically a piece of meat, potatoes, and cabbage, all cooked up together with lard in the pan on the gas stove and served onto the plate. That was it, never anything to follow. I don't recall anything like fruit in the house unless someone was ill. We didn't eat together as a family except on Christmas day, and if you were still hungry, you could "eat some bread."

I was sent to see the careers officer for Salford and when he asked me what I would like to do, I said that I would like to be a journalist as English was my best subject and I was an avid reader. I used to read all the Newspapers on my paper round, loved reading anything from the local Library, and felt confident that I could manage it. He said, "no lad you can't do that" and picking a card out of a file said, "here you are get down to Salford docks and ask for Captain Moore at Manchester Liners." Although my nerves showed when I met him, the Captain gave me the job to start immediately after my fifteenth birthday, for the princely sum of £15 per month.

Salford Docks in 1957 was a throbbing metropolis. There were three thousand five hundred people working there with nine docks, a railway – which ran with goods wagons – and the filthiest water one could imagine. It was reached by travelling down Trafford Road, which had dozens of cafes and pubs seemingly on every corner. My first morning, I was up bright and early and walked down Great Cheetham Street, along past Albert Park, and waited outside the Tower Cinema for the green Salford City Transport number 71 bus. I went upstairs because I was going to have a fag. In our house, there were seven people and six of us would eventually smoke.

When I tell people that at one time, we had a cigarette machine in our house, they don't believe me, but it is true. It was a mahogany box structure with four channels, one for Woodbines for mam, Players or Senior Service for dad, and Bensons or Rothmans King Size for the rest of us. A little Irish man called Jimmy Hill used to come every week to empty the money channels and refill the ciggy tubes.

I felt really grown up, puffing away as the bus travelled down Trafford Road, which was known locally as the 'Barbary Coast' and left me outside the giant white gates of the Manchester Ship Canal Company. There was a dock policeman permanently on the gate, and he directed me to the brick building, which was Manchester Liners. The company dealt almost exclusively with Canada and North America, the Ships were all called 'Manchester' something or other such as Manchester Miller, Manchester Venture, Manchester Vanguard sort of thing. They were proud of their reputation for 'turning round' a ship in a week, which meant one day up the Ship Canal, two days unloading, three days loading again and one day back down again to put to sea from the Mersey.

One thing that struck me as unfair even then was the system of employment. The Dockers who were not regular employees would stand every morning in a sort of a well. The foremen walked along a little wall which ran around the area where there could be as many as 500 men holding up their Docker's book, and if the foreman took your book you were working, if not you waited until lunchtime and if still nothing doing, you would have your card stamped and could go home.

My job was to be office boy, which meant making tea twice a day for twenty blokes. I worked in the general office and one thing that sticks in my mind is that of the twenty chaps there, sixteen, including me, used to smoke cigarettes. In the winter with the windows closed to keep the heat in, the fog was so thick that you were hard pressed to see across the room. In the 1950s everybody seemed to smoke, and I was no exception. My birthday was at the end of June, and I started work early in July, so I was an incredibly young fifteen year old. This didn't stop me from getting a bit cocky, especially with the crew members of the ships. Once a week I was given a docket from our catering department and took it to whichever ship was moored at number nine dock. This piece of paper entitled me to be given quantities of loose tea, sugar, and condensed milk, which I used for the brews. One day I gave a bit of cheek to the Chief Steward as he was weighing the tea. He warned me to watch myself, but I took no notice and kept winding him up. He and a couple of crewmen grabbed me and dangled me over the side of the ship by my ankles. A minute of this was enough to reduce me to terrified tears. It was never mentioned again, but my attitude to the chaps on the ships showed a marked improvement.

My duties included going round to number nine dock's warehouse to collect the checker's tally books, going to the café for toast at ten every morning, answering the phone to relatives of the sailors who were on our boats coming up the Manchester Ship Canal from The Mersey estuary, filing thousands of clerks' tally receipts and many other jobs. There was never enough time to catch up with my duties, and I just seemed to keep running as fast as I could to stand still. I settled well enough and was reasonably content with my lot. Each month I would hand over my pay packet and my mum would give me a pound a week spending money.

One of my main duties was to go each morning to a little window in an office in the giant Ship Canal building to collect what were known as 'ships movements'. These would tell me how a ship was doing coming up the canal, which would take a day. Then when the relatives called, I could tell them what time their spouses would arrive. One day my immediate superior said to me, "are you going to collect movements soon?" When I said yes, he told me to ask for the key to Mode Wheel Lock. I expressed some surprise but was assured that they needed it to use as a shortcut. I knocked on the window and after they had given me the slip of paper with the movements, I asked for the key to Mode Wheel Lock. The window closed for a second and I could hear a sort of snuffling noise from behind. When it opened again, the chap said that I had to go to the fifth floor, look for the office of Walter Preston Docks Manager and go right in, he was expecting me and would give me the key, which was in his desk. I was now quite excited, meeting the docks manager and me only 15. I called the lift and ascended to floor five; the executive floor and bypassing his secretary knocked and entered Mr Preston's palatial office. He looked at me with a face like thunder and asked me what I wanted.

"I've come for the key to Mode Wheel Lock Mr Preston," I said.

His face softened a little and he said to me, "key lock, key lock." It dawned on me that I had been the victim of a joke. Oh no, my face coloured blood red and I started stumbling my apologies, expecting instant dismissal. Mr Preston, bless him, gently pointed out that the date was the first of April, and sent me on my way. That took a lot of living down.

One great bonus for me was that being on the docks meant that I was only a mile from my beloved United at Old Trafford. Growing up in Broughton around the corner from the 'Cliff', their training ground meant that us kids could watch the team training whenever we liked. The players were on something like twenty pounds a week, so they were not so different from the average working man, but of course they were still our heroes. Matt Busby had fashioned a team of wonder boys as far as we were concerned, and I went to every game. My particular favourites were Eddie Coleman, a swivel-hipped son of Salford, Liam Whelan, who was reputed to be a distant cousin from Ireland, and of course the incomparable Duncan Edwards.

I had been there about six months – and on this cold February day – had just got back to the office with my checker's books. Obviously, something was up, someone who was supposed to know, came in and said that there had been a plane crash, but no injuries. As the afternoon dragged on and the true story emerged, we all became numb. The following days were a blur. Twenty-eight people had died, including eight players, Matt Busby was not expected to live, and Duncan Edwards was just clinging to life.

The sense of loss and of what might have been has never left me, nor has the feeling of absolute despair when Duncan died three weeks later. Part of the folklore of that time was the amount of people who went to the first match after Munich. I left work at 5.00pm and walked the mile to Old Trafford. The match was an FA cup game against Sheffield Wednesday, and never have I experienced such an emotional atmosphere. The programme, which I kept for years, had a series of blanks where the united team names should have been. Poor old Sheffield had no chance, and United were carried to victory on a tide of emotion.

My affection for United has never wavered. I had a season ticket for a while in the '60s. It was not expensive to go to the games in those days especially if like me, you went as a junior. My son has inherited my fervour, and one of my regrets was that when he was small, I could not afford to take him more than a couple of times a season. The prices by then had spiralled to ridiculous levels, pricing the working man out.

6: Amateur Days

At the youth club, we continued to do drama after a fashion, but this was not enough for me. I joined the local society, Salford Players, and found a whole new world. Here were people who felt like me about acting. I was given my chance early enough and played a part in the farce *Dry Rot*. When the opening night came around, my stomach turned the usual somersaults and I was as nervous as a kitten, but something amazing happened. Throughout the performance, people laughed. It is impossible to overstate the effect this had on me. I felt invincible. I had caused these gales of mirth. I was no longer inferior. I was a comic.

An old actor in this production was Cliff Cavanagh. He was a garrulous old chap and after one performance came into the dressing room waving an envelope that had a caricature of him and me sketched on it. He shouted, "look what Harold has done for me, I think I'll frame it." I thought he was making a fuss about nothing, and the scrawled signature on the bottom meant nothing to me. Who on earth was Harold Riley?

People at Salford Players spoke fondly of a young actor who had appeared briefly for them before applying to drama school. His name was Krishna Bhanjee, and he was supposed to have some ability. He apparently changed his name to Ben Kingsley. I wonder what happened to him?

This success made me more determined to follow what was becoming an obsession. Someone told me that Altrincham Garrick Theatre was the place to go if one wanted to act in good quality drama. The Garrick had a purpose built six hundred seater Theatre and a professional Director. I duly turned up and found that I had to audition before I could even be considered for roles. This I did and was almost immediately given a part, so someone must have thought I had something to offer. The following five or so years found me quite happily playing parts in all sorts of plays between the two societies, culminating in a lead role in a play called *Someone Waiting* by Emlyn

Williams. I had become much more confident in my ability, I felt at home on-stage, where I was happy and fulfilled.

In all the large cities at the time, there was a flourishing amateur theatre scene, and I have realised as the years have gone by, that there are a lot of exceptionally fine actors attached to them. For many reasons – mainly financial – people cannot afford to take the plunge in the profession and have had to content themselves with being an actor as a hobby. A case in point is our family Solicitor, who had been to see me both in straight plays and panto, and each time, told me that he would love to do what I am doing. He was a fabulous actor and a leading light at the Stockport Garrick Theatre, but had family and financial responsibilities. I have always said that if ever I had a 'proper' job, I would have given up acting years ago.

One good thing that came from Altrincham was that I stopped smoking. I had smoked all through my school days and by this time I was smoking sixty fags a day. This seems unbelievable – even to me – but in those days everybody, in film, television, and public life smoked. I had graduated from office boy to shipping clerk. My job was as boring as hell, no wonder we all smoked. I was doing a musical at the Garrick, directed by Paula Tilbrook, a very funny lady who I was to run across many times over the years. At times I could hardly breathe, and I knew my chest was starting to resemble my dad's. When I told everyone that I was stopping, even my mum said, "you'll never stop son, you smoke too much." Paula encouraged me, and the fags had gone. She had finished up in *Emmerdale* after a chequered career round and about the local reps and was as funny as ever.

By now, I knew that all I wanted to do was act. Members of both societies made regular trips to the big Manchester Theatres, the Palace and Opera House, and I remember being entranced by Lawrence Olivier as Shylock. As my Emlyn Williams play was nearing performance, I pestered a local actor's agent to come and see it. She was a fierce lady with a heart of gold and after seeing me and having an interview, she said that if I could get myself an Equity card, she would take me on.

If anyone wanted to appear on television in the 1960's even as a background artist, they could not do so without an actor's Equity card. Of course, because of this they were greatly prized, but the catch 22 was that you could not get a card unless you were already a professional actor. This seemed to put paid to my ambitions until someone told me that if you could get paid work in working men's clubs as a singer, you could be classed as a professional and could apply for a provisional card. Then after providing proof of six month's paid engagements you could make your card permanent.

Lots of the pubs around Salford at that time had entertainment in the form of a piano and drum combo and sometimes a compere who was usually a singer. As I could sing a bit, I started to try the talent competitions in the locals, and after a couple of months of terrifying myself, I started to control my nerves and found that I could chuck a few jokes into the mix and even get a few laughs. The aim was to get myself to a standard where I could hold my own as a club entertainer, get some paid bookings and obtain the all-important Equity card.

My first club booking was a disaster. It was fine being in a talent competition where nothing was expected but turning up at a club when you were the paid 'turn' was something else. If the audience did not like what you did, you were just ignored. It took a couple of months before I became proficient enough to stop trembling from the minute I arrived at a club, and to be honest I was now enjoying myself as well as earning some money. Reliable Club acts could find plenty of work.

My club persona was a strange hybrid. I did not want to be just a singer as there were hundreds around. My voice lent itself to songs from artists of that era especially Matt Monroe, Vince Hill or Perry Como. I would wait for acts like these to release a new record, get the sheet music and learn the words and tune within a day. This was unusual for the local club 'turns', and so when I would arrive at a club with up-to-date songs such as 'Edelweiss' by Vince, which was a big hit, or 'Softly as I leave you' by Matt, I was in some demand.

The musicians in the clubs were nearly always organists and drummers. Lots were self-taught and didn't read music, so the trick was to have as many 'numbers' as possible, so that if you let them choose the ones which they could play, you had a chance.

Almost all the time, I would be the only act on for that night, which meant that you were the total entertainment for the evening. Three half hour spots were the 'norm', and you invariably had to finish the evening with a 'dance' spot. This was for the audience to get up and dance before they went home and necessitated such standards as 'Amarillo', ' Ten Guitars', and 'Beautiful Sunday' to be trotted out. I lost track of the number of times that my patter would fall on deaf ears, and my 'serious' singing would 'die', only to be rescued by the last spot when everyone in the club was pissed, and danced deliriously.

My comedy started because of the success I had experienced in *Dry Rot*. I desperately wanted to have that feeling which came from making people laugh, so I learnt a few jokes, which I had stolen from acts like Bernard Manning, and slowly introduced them. Because I thought of myself more an actor than a club entertainer, I learned and practiced the gags as I would a script. The persona I adopted was a strange, almost ingratiating cross between a Les Dawson, and Old Mother Riley, which seemed to be working in the working men's clubs but would never allow me to go any further. I did not realise this at the time, I was just so pleased to be getting laughs and singing.

Looking back from a distance, I realise that to be a true comic, one would have to keep trying and writing new stuff and performing it. This required a lot more courage than I possessed, and I quickly acquired the comfort blanket of a set routine, which hardly varied from year to year.

I had bad nights of course, but also some memorable ones. I remember working at a giant club called Park Hall in Charnock Richard where the top of the bill was Cannon and Ball. They were the biggest thing in show business at the time, and there were 1400 people in that night. I had to do the opening spot and was trembling so much as I was announced, I thought the floor was vibrating. I sang my opening song and started my patter. At the front was a party of 20 women, who laughed uproariously at my first few gags. This gave me confidence, and I went from strength to strength, coming off after half an hour to a storm of applause.

This is it! I thought. I am a success. The following night I played to a crowd of 30, and 'died' the most miserable death, it did not do to get too big headed or complacent, you were only ever as good as your last show.

As my club career took off, I started to travel up and down the country, but always to working men's clubs.

Working at a rough club in Gorton, Manchester, I was on my last spot when two policemen came in. From the stage I could see them gesticulating, and the concert secretary pointing to me. When I finished, they came into the dressing room and asked me about my car. It had been stolen while I was on stage and the police had come across two men just about to take off the wheels. The men ran away, and the policemen found that I was the owner, phoned Helen who told them where I was working, and here they were. My car had been stolen and found without me knowing anything about it, they took me to it, and I drove home, how lucky was that?

7: Into Showbiz

I decided I would become a full-time entertainer and that Manchester Liners would have to get on as best they could without me. I left with few regrets, and I'm sure the feeling was mutual. I used to make a lot of mistakes when I reached the dizzy heights of shipping clerk, from office boy, and one still haunts me. The clerk's job was to copy the bill of lading from the checker's books, which the office boy collected twice a day, and then the goods would be loaded according to the clerk's bill of lading. This particular day, a car had been shipped to Vancouver instead of Florida, and a team of clerks was sifting the files to see how it had happened. As they got nearer to the bill in question, my sense of foreboding increased, with good reason because when they unearthed it, it was unmistakably my writing. A tremendous bollocking followed, and I was suitably contrite. I couldn't keep my mind on the job, and it was clear that no matter how long I stayed, I would never amount to much; so, I said cheerio and cleared my desk.

My mum was not too happy about my giving up a regular, reliable job, but by now I was my own man. How hard could this acting/entertaining lark be? Surely it would only be a matter of time before my talent was recognised.

I used always to read the *Daily Mirror*. I loved the column by 'Cassandra', but when there was a furore about his comments to do with Liberace, it went straight over my head. In that way, I had led a very sheltered life. Homosexuality was never mentioned, and I knew nothing about it. It must be said that I knew extraordinarily little about girls either.

What did attract my attention was a blurb about a new twice-weekly drama to be aired on the 9th of December 1960. It was set in a back street in Salford and was supposed to reflect some of the everyday trials and tribulations of working-class people. I watched, and quite enjoyed it. The next morning, the *Mirror* slated it saying it was so unrealistic, especially the part where young Barlow was mending his bicycle in the house. My bike was always in our hall, so I didn't know what he was going on about. They said it wouldn't last. I wonder if they'd like to revise their opinion?

With regard to my cabaret act, my long-term difficulty was that I settled into a working men's club act mentality. I would pinch and adapt jokes and patter that I had seen and add them to my comedy routines, but there was nothing original about me. Working men's clubs seemed to like quite rude jokes, and I never looked to drop the more risqué material, which served me so well in my present environment but would never get me into theatre or television comedy. Many a time I would come off after a good show, and people would say "you're miles better than we get on Telly", but that wasn't me, that was an actor playing the part of a Lancashire comic. I would earn a living, but never get any further. This was something I did not realise at the time, and it did not bother me in the least. I was enjoying myself and earning money. I was footloose and fancy-free, the world was my lobster!

I successfully applied for a post as a Redcoat at Butlins Holiday camp, and duly set off for Bognor Regis. As a child I had never been on holiday. The only outing we ever had was a day trip to Southport sponsored by the Salford Labour Party. To say I was excited at leaving home for the first time is an understatement. The South coast was a revelation; everything was bright, sunny and pristine.

Holiday camps at the time were pretty up market as far as I was concerned, and I settled quite happily into the routine of having breakfast with the holidaymakers and mixing with them until midnight when 'goodnight campers' sent us to bed exhausted. When I first put on the red jacket, I was really embarrassed. It took an effort to overcome my shyness and venture outdoors, I felt so conspicuous. However, the campers were quite nice, and after I got over my initial shyness, I enjoyed the camaraderie of my fellow 'coats'.

After a few weeks, as we were greeting the new intake one day, I saw a face I recognised. "Good God, it's Ronnie Clayton," I blurted in excitement. Ronnie was the captain of Blackburn Rovers football team and an England regular. He asked me not to tell anybody who he was because he wanted a quiet week with his family, and no one knew him down south. I kept his secret, and on the Friday night he thanked me and bought me a couple of pints. The thrill of sitting having a chat with Ronnie has never left me. He knew I was nervous but put me at my ease and I had an unforgettable evening. Those were the days when footballers would retire to buy a paper shop or a pub. Somehow, I can't see it happening now. Although I did get a chance to appear in the Redcoat show, Butlins was not what I wanted to do, and one season was enough.

I did lose my virginity though, to a chalet maid called Angela. Because my chalet also housed another redcoat, who had a girl with him, we had to go elsewhere, and ended up in a boxing ring in the deserted arena. All that fuss for two minutes.

By now I had the all-important Equity card and applied again to see if I could get Zena Sharpe to be my agent. She said yes, and warned me that as I was very inexperienced, I would have to start at the bottom and become an 'extra', to find my way around the TV studios. She got me my first job straightaway and I turned up at Granada studios to play a soldier in *Family at War*. On arrival I was sent straight to make-up and given a drastic short back and sides. I never had particularly long hair and so for me it wasn't too bad, but the arguments between extras and the powers that be, were legendary, many refusing to have their hair cut for what might only be one or two days' work. On one occasion, a Liverpool comic was persuaded to have his hair shorn with the promise of lots more work. In fact, when it came to his scene, he was covered by a blanket on a stretcher. He was playing a dead body!

My next job was three days at the newly opened Yorkshire TV studios.

Zena was looking out for me and job followed job. We used to travel from Manchester to Leeds for £6 per day, and this was before the M62 was built, and the journey would take us through Oldham and Huddersfield, a real pain. My first job was on a programme called Justice, starring Margaret Lockwood and, although she was incredibly old at the time, she was still a mega-star to us.

My next one at Leeds was a new show about two young and up and coming MPs played by William Gaunt and a young Michael Gambon. This was my first exposure to wonderful television acting. I had sneaked onto the set when not needed as an extra, and watched Gambon and Gaunt play a very intense, wordy scene. Every time they played the scene, they changed it slightly; never the dialogue, that was sacred, but they would give a slight change of emphasis for each take. I watched in wonder, realising at that moment, that no matter how long I would be in this business, I would never ever be a tenth as good as either. Of course, there could not ever be a parallel; how could you try to compare RADA, The West End Theatre, Royal Shakespeare company and leading Television roles, with my Salford Players and the amateur world? However, I wasn't unhappy, although I knew that I would never be more than a small part player or character actor that was what I was aiming for, and eventually became.

Our trips to Yorkshire TV were not always happy. I was booked to do the new daytime series, Emmerdale Farm, which was set in the countryside.

When I arrived, I found that I was one of fifty-five extras for a big market scene. The poor chap who was trying to keep us under control was out of his depth, and he had the bright idea of giving us all numbers to make it easier for him to call us out for the different shots. Of course, we all took umbrage at being numbered, and every time he tried to call us to the set, we all just milled around like sheep 'baa-ing' loudly. He panicked and screamed at us, but pandemonium ensued, and filming had to be curtailed. It was a classic example of how not to treat people, even if we were only extras. I vowed to stop doing extra work as soon as I could.

Coronation Street had been going for a couple of years by now, and my first appearance was in the Rovers. Although some people thought it was exciting, the reality of being an extra was dispiriting. We really were the lowest of the low and were looked down upon by everybody and very rarely addressed by any of the main cast. To be fair, a lot of extras brought this upon themselves. They could be quite bolshie and undisciplined, they were mainly retired people, or club artistes like me. Some, who were very well known in their own field, did not take kindly to being bossed around by younger floor managers.

Extra work was quite plentiful, and I worked on programmes like *Shabby Tiger*, *Sam* with a young Mark McManus, and *The Lovers* with Paula Wilcox and Richard Beckinsale. The money was a useful addition to my club earnings.

8: Mike & Bernie

My so-called career took a surprising turn round about now. Zena Sharpe phoned one day just before Christmas and told me there was an opening for a dresser in panto at the Davenport Theatre in Stockport with Mike and Bernie Winters. The last thing I wanted was to become a dresser, but as they were so famous, I thought I might as well go and meet them. They were delightful to me and made me feel welcome and important. I decided to take the job for a couple of months until the end of the panto. At that time Mike and Bernie were the second top double act in the country, and although they had many detractors, had millions of fans, and the stage door was always inundated with people waiting for autographs after the show.

I must say working for two such stars was a very enjoyable experience. I was entrusted with taking calls when they weren't about, or on stage. One such call came one Monday night in the middle of the show. When I answered it, the voice said, "Hello who is that?"

"I'm Jim, Mike and Bernie's dresser," I answered.

"OK Jim, this is Michael Grade, their personal manager. Tell them that I've fixed up that Palladium date and to call me back, cheers, goodbye."

I met Michael a few times and he always treated me with kindness and consideration. I also became friendly with their agent, Joe Collins, and as I was a pretty good tea maker from my days as office boy on Salford docks, shared many a brew while the 'boys' were on stage. It wasn't until many weeks later that I discovered that his family were the owners of the famous 'Collins Music Halls' in the early 1900s. Joe's daughters were Joan and Jackie Collins.

After a matinee one afternoon, there was a knock on the dressing room door, it was Mike Summerbee, the famous Manchester City footballer. He had his three-year-old daughter with him. Although Mike was from the 'other' team in Manchester, in those days there was no animosity between fans, just good-natured banter, and I was a bit overawed. His little girl kept asking where the panto 'horse' lived, and I offered to take her to see it while they talked important things like last night's match. We went down the steep backstage stairs to the chorus dressing room, and everyone made a fuss of her. She was so excited that when we reappeared, she just came out with a jumble of words to her dad about horsy lying down, ladies in pretty dresses, and 'Buttons' picking her up.

Mike and Bernie's Dad was a lovely old 'Yiddish' man who everyone knew as 'Mudgie'. Mudgie was a nickname that he had earned earlier in his life. It meant 'naughty boy', and he got it because of his connections to the gangs on the fringes of the criminal fraternity during the 1930s. He took to me, I think, partly as a link to his sons, who of course had their own lives to lead. When we worked in London, I stayed with him in his Highbury flat. He was a widower and we got on well. He insisted that we went to the local Jewish bakers on Sunday mornings for bagels, which he would warm in the oven. One midweek night Manchester City was playing Arsenal at Highbury, and as the boys did not need me, I decided to go to the match. As I was passing the massive entrance to the stadium amongst the vast crowd, a voice shouted: "Hey you Jim." Fifty of us turned around and it was Mike Summerbee "Where are you sitting? "He yelled at me. In those days' stadiums were not all seated and, as far as I was concerned, seats were for rich fans.

"I'm going to the cheap end Mike."

He pulled out a ticket for the director's box and said, "there you are, that's for looking after my little girl. She's never shut up about that pantomime horse lying down having a sleep."

At the end of the run in Stockport, Bernie asked if I would like to become their road manager and travel around with them. It was like being a second-hand star and although it wasn't what I really wanted, I thought that as very little was happening to me, I might as well give it a go.

A five-week tour was coming up and before the first week at Webbington Country Club in Western-Super-Mare, Bernie was having a party at his home in Berkshire for his wife Izzie's birthday. He asked if I would be barman for the evening. I was becoming quite a boozer now having picked up the habit from working on the docks, and I did not have to be asked twice. The house was magnificent and included a pool, tennis court, a sauna in the garden and a ballroom in the main wing of the house. All the current Arsenal football team were there, and although I was a Manchester United fan having been born around the corner from their training ground in Salford, I was thrilled to bits.

We were serving Champagne, but people could order what they wanted, and I spent an incredibly happy evening getting blotto with George Graham.

Bob Wilson made a big impression on me as he really gave me the feeling that he valued my opinion about things. He may have just been being kind, but nonetheless I have never forgotten it. Also, in attendance were Jimmy Tarbuck and Lionel Blair, and I had a good chat with Alan Ball.

In my new position as road manager, we set off on a five-week tour of the big cabaret clubs, starting at the Webbington, then to the Fiesta Sheffield, Fiesta Stockton, Fiesta Birmingham and finally the Golden Garter Manchester.

Working with Mike and Bernie for a year gave me an insight into the pressures and drawbacks, as well as the advantages of being stars. They could never just go to a pub for a quiet drink. Within minutes Bernie especially, would be targeted by people wanting autographs and pictures. This wasn't a particular problem – we always carried photos, and they would happily sign – but for some reason, people could be really objectionable, saying things like "sign it, it's for the wife", or "I think you're crap." One day Bernie and I were going to a football match in Cardiff, and the ground was about half a mile walk from the Angel Hotel where he was staying. He wore a cap and sunglasses and had wrapped a scarf completely round his face. We got no more than 20 yards before he was recognised.

Also, in Cardiff, the three of us were sitting in a café having a coffee when a little old lady hobbled up to us. Mike went to get his pen when the lady looked us up and down, pointed at me and said: "Are you Mrs Evans boy?" Bernie said, "I bet you get fed up with that."

As we settled into a touring routine, it became apparent that there were frictions. As with most double acts the straight man was often reviled as being the weaker or less talented part of the act. Mike was a fine musician who had studied at the Royal College of Music, and he liked nothing better than to have an impromptu jam session whenever we worked with good backing musicians. He tried not to show his hurt when thoughtless remarks were made, but there was no doubt that he felt the barbs.

They always stayed at separate hotels. Bernie loved to stay in 'theatrical Digs', because he liked the camaraderie of the other acts. I have to say that I idolised Bernie, I felt that he was a true 'clown', and he could easily reduce me to tears of laughter, even off stage. There was a famous theatrical digs in Leeds, where Bernie always stayed. It was owned by a formidable lady named Helen Bradley. We stayed for a week when appearing at Cinderella Rockefellas, which was owned by an up-and-coming impresario called Peter Stringfellow.

The landlady was rumoured to have a shady past, which may have included a stint as a 'Lady of the Night', but she ran a tight ship and many now famous acts had stayed. One whom she never tired of talking about was a singer whose original club name was Jerry Dorsey. He was at Helen's when his first record was on the powerful *Jukebox Jury*, it was voted a resounding 'miss', and he was in tears. The song was 'Release Me'; and the rest was history. Helen told me that she was with him when he decided to change his name to Engelbert Humperdinck, and she even called her little dog Engelbert. She was still a close friend of his, and towards the end of the week told me that Jerry had asked her to look out for a person who he might train up as his road manager. She said that she thought that I would be ideal, and would I like the job? Out of loyalty to the 'boys', I turned down the offer, and found out some years later that Engelbert Humperdinck's road manager had gone on to become a millionaire.

I never forgot that I was the hired help. I was always introduced to other acts as "Jim who's looking after us." We were in a bar one night at the Piccadilly Hotel in Manchester. Jimmy Tarbuck asked me: "What are you drinking Jim?"

I thought that I had better be a bit up market in such company and I said, "I'll have a small Southern Comfort please Jim."

He said: "You'll have a large one and like it while you're with us." I had a great night with them and never had to pay for a drink.

Joe Collins told me one day that with all double acts, one was always early and the other one was always late. I know it's a bit of a generalisation, but he was quite right, Bernie would always appear in the dressing room an hour before the show and Mike would often saunter in with 15 minutes to go. During the year and a half that I spent with them, I never heard an argument, and when they split up some time later, it seemed a shame.

I also learned something of their struggles during their early days. They were doing a matinee once at the notorious Glasgow Empire, they would start the act by Mike coming on stage playing his Clarinet, Bernie would pop his head round the curtain and say "eeeeeee", and off they would go. This afternoon, there were two chaps sitting in the second row, one reading a newspaper and taking no notice as Mike played. When Bernie stuck his head out the man put down his paper and turned to his mate saying, "Oh Christ, there's two of them."

The day of the band call at the Golden Garter, the boys had to appear on a television programme to publicise their upcoming TV series and asked me at short notice to take the band rehearsal. Although I was nervous, I had seen all the band calls on the tour, and I knew the act backwards. The bandleader was a very pleasant chap called Pete Brown who made me feel at home. I seemed to acquit myself well and the show went like clockwork, the boys were pleased and from then on, I took the band calls unless it was an especially important show. This made me feel a lot better about the job as I now felt more than just a 'roadie '.

An upcoming charity engagement was at the London Palladium on a Sunday. We were in the Isle of Man the previous week, and there was no chance that Mike and Bernie could get from there to London after the Saturday show for the rehearsal. They sent me ahead on the Saturday to take the band call. The show was in front of the Duke of Edinburgh and among the cast were Cleo Laine and Johnny Dankworth, Leslie Crowther and the cast of the current west end hit *Godspell*. The bandleader was Jack Parnell and he had an Orchestra of about 50 musicians. He insisted that he needed me to go through the cues of the act on-stage, and so I can always say that I appeared on the stage at the London Palladium with a 50-piece orchestra.

Towards the end of the year, I realised that although it was exciting and different working for the boys, I really wanted to do my own thing, and reluctantly gave in my notice. They were off to do a 12-week panto in Coventry, and I really did not want to go back to being a dresser for 12 weeks. They accepted that I wanted to do my own thing and we said goodbye. I will never know how things would have turned out if I had stayed, but I now knew that 'stars' were ordinary people with just as many insecurities as the rest of us.

Just before finishing with them, I mentioned that I would love to do a Panto, and Bernie kindly made a phone call and got me a meeting with a big impresario who was casting for several shows at a London theatre. I sat in line at the audition and when there were only two of us left, the chap came out and gestured for us both to go in. I thought it was a bit peculiar but entered with the other chap. Throughout the ten-minute meeting the impresario didn't address one word to me but simply engaged the other fellow in conversation and gave him a job in – of all places – Manchester.

Then he said to him, "Off you go and take your friend with you."

He retorted "I've never seen him before in my life." I had done it again, sat through someone else's full interview. I was so embarrassed; I left the theatre and told no one.

9: At Last, a Professional!

Back home, I returned to the grind of working men's clubs and tons of extra work. I was becoming more and more unhappy that all that seemed to be on offer was background stuff.

Don't get me wrong; I had some lovely experiences in clubs. Once when I was doing a week in Liverpool, I turned up at a club to find that the backing was a seven-piece jazz band. I was a bit flustered as my music consisted only of piano and drum parts, but the leader whose nickname was 'snowy' told me not to worry, as they would extemporise behind me. They were brilliant and I had a smashing night. When I mentioned it to a fellow act, he told me that they were well known in Liverpool as the 'Saturated Seven', and 'Snowy' was Joe Royle's dad. I always thought that if I ever met Joe, I would tell him what a gentleman his dad was.

My agent phoned me one day and told me to get down to the newly formed Contact Theatre in the university buildings in Manchester. One of the cast of their opening production of the *Knight of the burning Pestle,* had dropped out at the last minute and they needed someone to learn the part and be ready to go on in four days. I got the job and joined a gang of incredibly talented people in the final stages of rehearsal. If I had had time to think about it, I might have been terrified, but as everything went by in a blur, I just got on with it. At last, I was a professional actor, and I made such an impression at Contact that I was asked to appear again just 20 years later. It meant the world to me; it gave me the 'Validation', which I desperately needed to boost my self-esteem, and was an important landmark. If I could hold my own with professional actors, perhaps I could make my way in the business.

The play started with me as grocer George, and my 'wife,' sitting in the audience. After about five minutes, I had to cause a disturbance, say that the play was rubbish and was invited on stage to see if I could do better. Most nights this was fine, but on a couple of occasions, we were the subject of 'tutting' from audience members who thought that we really were spoiling the play, and one night a bloke said that if I didn't shut up, he would punch me. I had to whisper that I was part of the play; I hope he wasn't too embarrassed.

Among the cast was a chap named David Ross. David used to put pictures of big-busted ladies in his script, which he maintained helped his concentration. We got on well, and a couple of years later he was playing at Contact in a new play called *Having a Ball,* by a new writer, Alan Bleasdale. The play was set in a working men's club and, knowing that I was a club act, David asked if I would come and watch a rehearsal and tell them if I thought anything was wrong. I did so, mentioned a few things that did not ring true and met Alan who was very nice, and I enjoyed the play. David played a part in Bleasdale's terrific series *Boys from the Blackstuff* and went on to the National Theatre and many TV roles.

In my role at Contact, my agent Zena persuaded a radio producer to come and see the show. His name was Tony Cliffe, and he engaged me for a couple of radio plays to be taped in Leeds. Radio was bliss, no lines to learn, working with people like Martin Jarvis and, on one occasion, a young Robert Powell. In the pub after the show, Robert confided that he was under consideration for a big role, which might help his career. The role was the name part in *Jesus of Nazareth,* which catapulted him to fame. My radio work on the other hand catapulted me to obscurity.

A salutary tale next, which still hurts me forty years on. Zena told me to go to the Victoria Theatre in Salford to meet Aubrey Phillips, who was casting a panto in which he was producer, director, and dame. The Victoria was a giant, ornately finished, century old building, which was used as a cinema, except at Christmas, when for a couple of months, it was a theatre venue. Aubrey Phillips had successfully run the panto there for some years, and I thought that I had a good chance of a part, considering my club, and TV experience.

The foyer was quite grand, and a little old lady was mopping the floor. She reminded me of my mam and greeted me warmly. She asked me to wait a moment and she would tell Mr Phillips I had arrived. A little, rotund man came out of an office, looked at me for about three seconds, and disappeared. The little lady reappeared, approached me and said, "I'm really sorry son, but the job has gone." I protested that I had not even been interviewed, but she insisted that I was wasting my time, and would I please leave.

I don't think I've ever been so hurt and embarrassed to be dismissed and told to go by the cleaning lady.

I went to the pub and got pissed.

A week later, I was to meet John Schlesinger, who was filming a Second World War epic to be called *Yanks*. The part I was up for was unspecified, as he liked to meet actors before casting the small parts. I waited in the interview room for two hours before being informed that Mr Schlesinger was too busy to see me and would rearrange. I heard no more.

Without any audition, my next telly was in the massive Granada series *Country Matters*. I was engaged as a non-speaking walk-on category two. This meant a £20 increase in my fee, and I would be classed as a 'directed extra'. My job was to spend the day snogging on the bed as the boyfriend of one of the main characters. By now my teeth were like pearls, I cleaned them so often, and I made a special effort that day with chewing gum and breath freshener. When we arrived on set, the girl said, "well we might as well get on with it," and we settled down to a day of snogging. The director was Michael Apted, and I often wonder if he has any memory of that 'directed extra', who spent a blissful day on the bed with one of his stars. For the first time, I was treated with some consideration on set. Michael was kindness itself and made a nonentity feel wanted.

It seemed as if I was considered now by the powers that be, to be more exalted than an extra. My next invitation was to appear in an epic for Yorkshire TV called "*The Glory Boys*" starring Rod Steiger and Anthony Perkins. Although there were no lines, I was to be the chauffeur in several scenes to be shot at Manchester Airport, and was once again to be a 'directed extra'.

The distinctions and differences in the world of background artists were myriad and labyrinth, and each promotion was jealously guarded. The lowest and most common was a basic extra, next came 'directed extra' when a person had some action to perform. Higher still was 'directed extra with special skills', when the action had some bearing on the drama taking place such as driving, horse riding, or say, skiing. Top of the heap was 'speaking walk on' and really exalted would be a 'speaking walk on with special skills'. Because of the difficulties of obtaining an Equity card, and the fact that no one could appear without it, there were people who made a living out of background work and very often a 'speaking walk on,' would look with disdain on a mere 'extra'. I, of course, was a 'proper actor', and used to look down on myself, consoling my deluded young self that this was just a temporary residence among the 'underlings' of the TV and film hierarchy.

Maggie Thatcher would soon put a stop to all this 'closed shop' business, and after her government declared the 'closed shop' illegal, anyone could appear, Equity card or not. Whilst I recognise the absurdity of the old system, since it has been opened up to anyone, filmmakers, trading on the public's desire to be on film or telly, have exploited people mercilessly.

Back to Manchester Airport with Mr Steiger and Mr Perkins, I was to drive a lovely Jaguar around a deserted stretch of runway, whilst someone was trying to assassinate Rod Steiger. No one had any dealings with either of them; they were ensconced in a Winnebago and would just appear as someone was about to shout" action", and then disappear. I revelled in my newfound status as a 'directed extra' and enjoyed an interesting week.

The film itself was a disaster for Yorkshire Television, costing a reputed three million pounds; a prohibitive amount for a TV film in those days. When it was broadcast the viewing figures were derisory, and the reviews not much better.

10: Early Corrie

A couple of months after my spell at Contact, I had a rare bit of excitement. Zena called and told me I had an audition at Granada for a speaking part in *Coronation Street*. I was met at the Studio entrance and taken to the casting department on the third floor. My knees were knocking, and I was trembling when I went in to be interviewed by the director June Wyndham Davies, and because I was so nervous, I did not feel I read very well. As the part was for a bumbling idiot who went into the corner shop to ask for corn plasters, they probably thought that a bit of typecasting was in order and I got the part. From now on, there would be no more background work and I was bursting with happiness. I knew that the chances of ever becoming more than a bit part player, or small part character actor were remote, but I didn't care, I was on the shaky ladder; it was enough.

In those days the cast of Corrie was the equivalent of pop stars and the programme was watched regularly by up to 20 million people. The fact that there were only two episodes a week and only two TV channels meant that choice was a bit limited. Although there was not a 'paparazzi' as such in those days, the core cast of Corrie was only about fifteen actors, and they couldn't walk about in public without being treated like film stars.

My four lines meant a week's work and I reported to the Granada building. As I walked up to the reception, the chap on the security desk, a commissionaire, jumped up and opened the door for me. I thought *hello I could get used to this*, but then he spoiled it by saying: "Oh I thought you were Michael Parkinson." Michael used to do Film Night from there in those days.

The difference when one had a speaking part was astonishing. I was met at reception by a second assistant director, escorted to the fifth floor, and introduced to everybody. We were in a cavernous rehearsal room, and the 'sets' were marked out on the floor with 'gaffer tape'. Sitting around, or going through their lines were Violet Carson, Peter Adamson, Pat Phoenix,

Bill Roache, and Philip Lowrie. They all said hello, and went back to their conversations, but I was made up, and could not wait to get home and tell mam.

On Monday, we rehearsed all day, and Tuesday the same. The cast were a bit distant and very business-like but as far as I was concerned, I was in wonderland, in the same room and chatting with the likes of Peter Adamson and Violet Carson.

Wednesday morning everyone seemed a bit dressed up and I soon found out why. The technicians, cameramen, sound people, and most importantly of all, the top brass in the form of producers and executives came into the rehearsal room and watched a run through of both episodes. When we got to my bit, they laughed so much we had to stop and have a tea break. Maybe they were just laughing at my hapless character, but I didn't care, it seemed as if I was not out of place in this environment.

Thursday the whole circus decamped, downstairs to the giant Studio six where the sets were built, and spent all day blocking and rehearsing camera, lighting, and sound cues. This was the most boring day, but they had to be meticulous and every single person, including actors, technicians and cameramen, had to know their exact position at any given moment.

Friday, the tension was palpable; we were to record one episode in the morning and the second after lunch. The episodes in those days had to be recorded in blocks of 12 minutes, which formed one half of an episode. They would have to go directly from one scene to the next without stopping, and if you arrived at 11 minutes and someone – not just an actor, but sound, or a cameraman screwed up – we would have to go back to the beginning and start again. The tension as the recording went on was unbelievable; certainly, I had never known anything like it. Needless to say, I was in a blue funk as my four lines approached. My task was to enter the corner shop, hit my mark exactly, and say my four lines to Elsie Tanner and Rita Fairclough. In the top of the door was a metal spike, this hit a bell as the door opened, causing a noise. It had gone askew, and as I opened the shop door; the bell did not ring. I knew this wasn't my fault but still it threw me, and I stumbled through my lines, thinking that I had spoiled the whole thing. I was mortified, the twelve minutes came to an end and nobody said anything to me. Everybody appeared satisfied and when I saw the episode three weeks later a 'ding' had been added to make the shop bell ring. So ended my first speaking part on British television. It did give me an insight into the pressures of performing week after week to such high standards. I had four lines and was wiped out afterwards, no wonder some high-profile performers did not last. One of the extras, a girl I knew who was a club 'turn' from Yorkshire, came up and said, "well done kid, that was really funny, you never know, you might get kept on." That was nice of her; her name was Liz Dawn, the next time I met Liz, I picked her up in my taxi to take her to the studios, by then she was Vera Duckworth.

Back to the clubs, if I thought my Corrie part would attract anyone's attention, I was sadly mistaken and I found myself quite depressed, having been treated like a 'somebody' for a few days and now ignored again. I thought that my appearance might have generated some interest in me, but what happened, was... nothing.

11: Crown Court

A welcome boost to my finances happened next. I was booked to play the Jury Foreman in Crown Court, the Granada afternoon programme that showed a trial in which the Jury, made up of members of the public, decided the verdict.

Because of Equity, the actor's union rules, the Foreman had to be an actor, as he had to speak to deliver the verdict. The programme ran for three consecutive afternoons; we the jury after watching the trial play out, retired to consider our verdict. After we had decided, we were brought back to the set to run through both decisions, before we readied ourselves for the 'take'. Nobody in the Studio except the jury knew the real outcome. I was warned not to say anything, especially to the actors, who wanted their performances to be spontaneous. The whole company, actors, cameramen, soundmen etc bristled with nervous excitement. It was rumoured that little bets were struck as we readied ourselves. "Will the jury foreman please stand" my knees knocked a bit, all eyes upon me, "do you find the defendant guilty or not guilty?"

"Not guilty", I said.

The court erupted into joy from the defendant, and there were angry mutterings from some of the public who disagreed with the verdict.

I had had a lovely week but imagine my joy when I got my cheque a couple of weeks later. Equity had insisted that as the foreman was booked as a named actor, I had to be paid for all the three episodes in which I appeared, even though I had only spoken in one. No complaints from me, hee hee.

12: Oldham Rep

Just before Christmas 1971, Zena called me to say that Oldham Rep had a problem. Alan Moore, a fine actor, who was to play the part of Buttons in their panto, had been cast as a main character in a new TV programme and would have to miss the opening week. They were trying to find someone who would rehearse the part and play it for just one week. As usual. I fitted the bill as 'super sub' and presented myself.

This was a terrific opportunity for me. We rehearsed for a week, and despite the usual opening night nerves, once we opened, I was in paradise. My job as Buttons to excite the kids, and try to get them to shout a response. I was tense and unsure, as I shouted "Hiya Kids", but was rewarded by six hundred screams of "HIYA BUTTONS". My heart swelled, this was what I had been searching for and from that moment, I fell in love with Panto.

I adored performing to the kids, sometimes six hundred of them. I could sing because of my club experience, and I found that my comedy went down very well. It was hard saying goodbye after only one week, but the artistic director, John Jardine, promised that he would keep me in mind for the following year.

Back to the club life, I forgot about the promise of returning to Panto next year, I had heard it all before. John though, was as good as his word and booked me to play 'Billy Crusoe' for Panto in 1972. This time, I had the full five weeks rehearsal, and the show ran for nearly twelve weeks. I first met and became friendly with Roy Barraclough, who played Dame, Peter Dudley who went on to play Bert Tilsley in Corrie, before dying tragically young, and a teenage Anne Kirkbride, who lived in Oldham and used to come into the bar. Although it was tiring to play twice nightly for such a long time, I can honestly say that I enjoyed every minute.

Roy Barraclough was quite a star at the time, appearing in *Pardon my Genie*, a children's programme, and the *Sez Les* show with Les Dawson. Les was at his absolute peak at this time, and the side-splitting moment in all the shows was his sketch with Roy as 'Cissie and Ada'. I told him how much I liked Les, especially as he had spent years doing the rounds of working men's clubs 'dying on his arse', before his confessional type of humour came into fashion. I particularly loved the story Les told about himself. Appearing at Lower Kersal Social, a big club in Salford, he was rambling on – as he does – and there was complete silence. Then a woman started laughing, only to be told by her husband, "hey shurrup there's someone talking." One afternoon in between shows, Roy sent for me to go to his dressing room. When I went, there was Les who had come to see the show. Roy had told him that I liked his stuff, and we had a cup of tea and a chat, Les was one of those comics who was just as funny off stage, and we did not stop laughing for an hour.

'Corpsing' is when you cannot stop laughing on stage. It is a nervous reaction to something often quite innocuous, but when it gets you, there is nothing you can do. I was sharing a dressing room at the rep with an actor called Alan Gaunt, who was playing the villain. Alan had graduated from RADA and was considered a serious actor. He particularly asked me not to try to 'corpse' him, which I never did. In the panto cast, was a girl who had come straight from *Jesus Christ Superstar* in London. She was extremely attractive and kept herself to herself. Halfway through the run, we decided to have a big party as we were in a bit of a lull, this happened in all long running shows, and was just a way of cheering ourselves up. Our 'superstar' girl got drunk and was wandering round asking people if they fancied a 'Donald Duck'. I had a girlfriend with me, and had to decline her kind invitation, but after asking nearly everybody in the cast, including Roy Barraclough, she finally arrived at Alan, whose eyes lit up and they disappeared, much to our amusement.

The following day, we were all on stage with an audience of six hundred and hangovers you would not wish on a dog. Alan, as the villain, had to go up to the dame and looking at the panto cow, demand, "you, you old crone, what's that?"

Roy, the dame, was in like a flash, "well it's not Donald Duck anyway, luvvie." Alan's mouth twitched, but he was so serious that he bit his hand until it bled. Roy wouldn't let him off the hook, "what's the matter chuck, doesn't it look like Donald duck? Don't you fancy her?" Poor Alan was now hopelessly lost. He screamed with laughter and could not say a single word. Disgracefully the whole show stopped as every single person on stage collapsed laughing. Fortunately, the audience seemed to like it just as much as us, and for two or three minutes you had the unprecedented spectacle of six hundred people and a Panto cast just laughing for no apparent reason. It was glorious absurdity and something, which is remembered fondly from a distance.

In any stage show, the company soon merge into a 'family'. This is especially true in Panto, when you have twelve weeks of going through the same emotions, trying your best to get as many laughs and reactions from the audience as possible, and helping each other. I was entranced by the children's reactions and would sometimes watch through the peephole in the proscenium arch to see the first couple of rows while waiting for my entrance. Little ones would start off a bit frightened, this might be their first ever visit to the theatre. They would hear other maybe older ones booing the villain, and soon realise that they could do it also. By the time I came on as Billy Crusoe, they were ready to scream support for me. This warmed my heart; I could forget everything and just be Billy for three hours.

When the panto finished, John employed me in a role in the next drama production, and when this finished asked if I would like to take part in a Music Hall later in the year. The show was to consist of two distinct halves. We the company would do the first hour as a music hall and the second half was to feature the newly famous Barbara Mullany who was a terrific singer. In the music hall section, I played the old pot man who made a nuisance of himself throughout the proceedings, and then in response to the audience's pleadings, well orchestrated by me, did a short comedy spot and sang 'My Old Dutch'.

Barbara started her acting career in Oldham and used to regale us with tales from weekly rep when actors would be playing one part in the evening, rehearsing next week's play during the day, and learning their lines for the following week when they went to bed. No wonder she had no trouble learning her lines for Corrie. The show was an enormous success and was Barbara's way of saying thank you to Oldham where she had learned her craft.

Anne Kirkbride appeared in the show dressed as a schoolgirl and sang 'Daddy wouldn't buy me a bow wow'. I wish I had some photos of that. I think a spot of blackmail might be in order.

During the rehearsals for the Music Hall, I met an actor named David Williams. He was a good actor and fine music hall performer, and we became and remain great friends. Every actor needs someone to confide in and have a good moan about why they are not working more, and why on earth someone else got that job. For forty years, we spoke once a week and put the acting world to rights.

Zena phoned one day and said, "Darling I've had Granada on the phone, they are absolutely desperate for people to play MPs in a gigantic House of Commons scene. It's only extra work and I know you don't do that anymore, but they said they would be very grateful if you would do it just this once." Reluctantly I agreed and turned up at the studios. The scene that greeted me was absolute chaos: Two hundred men were getting changed into suits to become MPs, the room was full of club acts, especially funny Scousers, and I wished I had said no.

I always went for a pee before going on set, and when I was washing my hands, the floor manager Peter Shaw came in: "Hello Jim, what are you doing among the extras?" This made me feel even worse, as he knew me as a 'proper' actor.

We went on set, a fantastic mock-up of the House of Commons, and sat for two hours while they started shooting. I was trying to stay awake when some sort of hiatus occurred. I could hear Peter saying into his mic, which connected him to 'upstairs', the director's gallery. "Yes, I know, we need someone to become an MP and swear the oath, or the scene doesn't make sense." After a few more urgent asides, Peter turned to the assembly of 'MPs' and said, "Could Jim Whelan please come onto the floor?" All eyes were on me as I arrived. "Jim, we've made a cock-up here, and we need you to ad-lib a few lines, and then read the oath of loyalty to the Queen from this card. Do you think you can manage it?"

Not even any time for nerves, this time I really was doing them a favour, I made up a couple of trite observations, read the oath, and we had it in one. So, for the wrong reasons, I had done the right thing and my contribution was upgraded to a 'speaking part'. Thank you, Peter.

13: A Well-Deserved Lesson

Around this time, an agent from Leeds had seen me and told me that if I left Zena Sharpe and signed with him, I would get a lot more work as he was inundated with enquiries for characters like me. I was flattered and told Zena that, after ten years, it was time to move on. She was terribly upset, but to my shame I told her that my mind was made up. She said that she would not stand in my way, but I could never come back. I joined the high-flying agency with the great contacts.

The phone didn't ring for two years.

I had made a catastrophic mistake.

I tried desperately to try to get Zena to take me back, but she refused. She maintained that if actors thought that they could just leave on a whim, and then return, she would never keep her clients. I am sure that she was right. It was a hard, but well-deserved lesson.

Looking back, I wonder if my treatment of Zena was shabby? No doubt that I got what I deserved, but my head was turned by the flattering blandishments of a bigger, more famous agency. Things had been quiet on the job front and my confidence had taken a hit. However, Zena had given me my start and became a friend. I did feel bad, I never spoke to her again and that hurts me. Had my ambition caused me to make the wrong decision or had I made what might eventually prove to be the right move? If I had stayed, would I be any better off, I suppose I can never really answer that question, but I do regret the loss of a friend.

14: Helen

I was now into my thirties, gently drifting along and becoming one of the lads in my local pub, giving no thought whatsoever to any sort of coherent future. I was working mid-week as a compere in a big local hotel and going off to do clubs at the weekend for better fees. As I was a single man, still living at home when I was not travelling around, the money I could earn from clubs and bits of telly, was enough to live on, and I was doing something I enjoyed.

One midweek night, I noticed a new barmaid had started and wondered if she might go out with me. It turned out that she was a teacher in Stockport and had decided to do a barmaid job to get her out of her flat a couple of nights a week. She was a lovely little girl and much too good for me, but I screwed up my courage and decided that if I were to have any chance, I would have to invite her to do something different. I asked if she might go to the theatre with me. Luckily, she accepted. Over the next few months, as we got to know each other, I became increasingly aware that Helen was the girl I wanted to spend my life with. I was in love. I had never really been a ladies' man, although some success had been mine along the way. My deep-down lack of confidence frightened me. I wanted to propose, but if she said no, I would walk away. One day in the pub, I blurted out "if I asked you to marry me, what would you say"? What a proposal! Fortunately, she could see through me, recognising my stupid shortcomings and said, "I'd say yes".

That was it. I was happy and relieved. We told Helen's dad and my mum and started planning.

We were married on Halloween in 1975. The reception was in the Heaton Park Hotel where we met, and both worked part-time. The lovely Edna and George, who ran the place, gave us a great reception in the Banqueting suite and it amazed me to see so many friends there. John Comer from Last of the Summer Wine was among the guests and David Ross, who was making a name for himself in TV also came.

We recently celebrated our 45th wedding anniversary, this was undoubtedly my best ever decision. Over the years, she has put up with my spectacularly unsuccessful career and continued teaching, only having a break when the children were small.

Applying for a mortgage on a semi in Bury, it brought home to me what a pariah I was for daring to be an entertainer. The building society manager told me very sniffily that my earnings were too 'mercurial', and he would not grant us a mortgage. Helen's dad however liked me and informed the building society that he would stand as a guarantor for the payments. I was thirty-three years old and the only way I could get on the property ladder was with the help of my future father-in-law.

I had never given any thought to having children, so when Helen announced that she was pregnant; I was not sure how I would cope. In the event, when my son Andrew was born, my life changed. I had never experienced unconditional love before, and I could not wait to get home to see him at anytime. Whatever kind of a day I had suffered, he could make me happy by launching himself at me as soon as he saw me.

A year and a half later, he was joined by a red headed, angry looking, and loveable little bundle who we named Lucy. Over the following forty or more years, they have been the antidote to anything bad that may have happened to Helen and me. Perhaps it might have been some kind of reaction to the mostly indifference I received from my own father when I was small, but my two have been my great joy since I set eyes on them, and they still are.

Helen wanted to take some time off when the children were small, and I had started to drive a taxi as we had a mortgage to pay. It was only intended as a temporary measure, but as TV jobs were becoming more and more scarce, I drove my taxi on and off between engagements for the next 25 years. I taxied during the week and continued my club work at weekends.

One day at home, a lamp started flickering. I grabbed it without unplugging it, could not let go and was electrocuted, flying around the room until the cord broke. I was left in a bad way with wounds to my hand, which the hospital emergency department told me would not heal for a month.

I had a booking the next night in Bolton and decided to go because we needed the money. When I arrived at the dressing room at the club, the other 'turn' was already there, a thickset man smoking a fag. "Bloody Hell what happened to you?" he asked. When I told him, he said that three weeks before he had had a heart attack whilst on stage but had continued to perform because – like me – he needed the money. He also told me that he did bits of extra work at Granada to earn some cash. His name was Bill Tarmey and of course went on to great fame as one of the best loved characters in Corrie; Jack Duckworth.

Some years later, I opened a shoe shop and one day, just before opening, the phone rang. "I've heard you're opening a shop. Do you want me to come along?" It was Bill.

"Well, I'm a bit skint," I said.

"Who said owt about money? I'll see you on the day."

He was as good as his word and turned up at the opening with loads of photos, which he signed for people, ensuring that the day was a great success and proving that nice guys do exist in the business. When we have met over the years in the Corrie green room, he always likes to recall our first meeting in a scruffy club in Bolton.

I played my first vicar in a daytime soap called *Families*, it was a nice little part, but the only abiding memory was of the boy playing the rebellious son. He was absolutely gorgeous, and whichever way the camera filmed him he looked good. His name was Jude Law, wonder what happened to him?

15: Postie in Corrie

Having had over twenty-five years of working in clubs, many things stick out in my mind. One Saturday night I was booked into Windle Labour Club, St Helens. The girl singer who was the other act was already in the dressing room. Whilst we were saying hello, an old chap who must have been at least 80, barged in with a large suitcase.

I said: "Hello! Who are you?"

"I'm Jim Whelan," he said. "Who are you?"

It seemed that he had been a well-known name in club circles around the Wigan area for many years and was now retired. He had been looking in the local paper and had seen the name Jim Whelan appearing at Windle Labour and had phoned to ask if this was correct as he did not remember making the booking. The concert Secretary said that he was definitely on and so here he was.

The concert secretary was a decent chap and because of the unheard-of circumstances, decided to call an immediate committee meeting. They decreed that they would pay him a fee and let him just do a short spot in the middle of the evening. The girl singer opened the show and had a moderate response, as this was a very hard club to work. I followed and fared not much better. The other Jim Whelan went on. He opened with the soldier's farewell, an old First World War number, and started his comedy patter with, "the wife will kill me when I get home, and she thinks I've only gone for a shit." He proceeded to bring the house down, so much so, that the girl singer and I had to shorten our acts in the second half so that Jim could do another spot. He was a lovely old chap and apologised to us for disrupting our evening. He had no need as he entranced us. He went on to tell me stories about his many years in the business, how he had started out as a singer in theatres and moved into clubs when they started to close. In the course of the evening, he mentioned his son Dave, who he said had started to sell trainers and stuff on

Wigan market and now appeared to be doing quite well. Dave Whelan, now where have I heard that name before?

Every actor has plenty of hard luck stories, how they were just beaten to a part etc., and I am no exception. One day I was called for an audition for an advert to be the new 'Unigate milkman'. I know that I have a funny face and sometimes this can go in my favour. This is what happened, and I was chosen from a motley crew of dozens. The shoot was in London and as is the way with adverts, money seemed to be no object. I was put up at a top hotel and chauffeur driven to the location. As we started shooting, the clients arrived, and I felt a sinking sensation when they started arguing and gesticulating with the director. Although I could not hear what they were saying, it was obvious that they were unhappy with me and the director reluctantly told me that they thought I looked too young. He replaced me with an actor who was on the shoot as an extra, Peter Martin. I still received my fee for the day and thought no more about it. Many years later, Peter Martin went on to star in tons of programmes including *The Royle Family* as Joe, the neighbour, and became a regular in *Emmerdale*. When I met him whilst filming *Emmerdale*, I asked him how things had panned out with Unigate, and he told me that he had been retained for many years as the milkman, and had earned something in the region of six figures. Because the ads were not shown in the Manchester area, I knew nothing about it. Perhaps it is just as well?

I auditioned again for *Coronation Street*, and got the part of the postman on the street. There was a regular extra who was the postie, but it seemed that whenever there were lines to say, they did not trust him. As I was now considered to be a seasoned performer, and fitted the uniform, I was booked. The Postman cropped up about half a dozen times over the next couple of years – never with many lines – and used mainly as a plot device, such as when Ken Barlow had moved, and someone had to find him, the Postie would ask one of the residents where he had gone.

The advantage from my point of view was that I would not have to audition for this particular 'job, it was a guaranteed job when required.'

In one of the episodes, I had to deliver the news of a windfall to Jack and Vera Duckworth. Vera grabbed me in an embrace because she was so grateful. I had first met Liz Dawn who played Vera, when we were both extras in a thing called *Shabby Tiger*. Liz was a club singer from Yorkshire, and through a combination of being in the right place at the right time, and transmitting her personality through the character, played Vera for many years. I picked her up more than once in my taxi during the following few years, and she was never less than gracious and generous.

One person on 'The Street', whom I was not so fond of was Johnny Briggs. I came on set one day to find him roundly berating a poor props man. "Where is my fucking Winnebago?" he shouted. The poor man was obviously in fear for his job and could not answer back. This went on for several minutes and left a terrible atmosphere with the cast and crew. I decided that I would steer well clear of him.

After auditioning, I got three lines in *The Liver Birds* as a policeman. As we were filming a woman came up to ask me directions, I did my best, but I think I sent her the wrong way. Ah well.

The following year, I was booked for another episode of *Liver Birds*. This time as a butcher. We were filming outside in an ordinary street. Polly James and Nerys Hughes were leading a march against animal cruelty, and my line was "get your knickers down." I nearly got lynched by a group of Scouse ladies who thought that I was a real butcher, ruining the shot.

Another audition got me the first of four appearances as different characters in *Last of the Summer Wine.* My visits were spread over many years and the cast was always changing as the main people died off. In my latest appearance a year ago, one of my heroes Peter Sallis said to me "who are you"?

I said, "I'm the church warden who's going to stop you lot parking that truck at the church."

"Oh crikey, I've got lines with you. Well don't expect me to know them. I'm too old you know, I'm eighty bloody eight." In fact, he was line perfect although he was very frail and had to be helped all the time by a nurse, but once the director said "action", he seemed to come to life. What a professional.

People's knowledge of, and loyalty to, television programmes, is always a source of amazement to me. The producer's assistant who greeted me when I turned up for my last 'Summer Wine' appearance said," Hello Jim, you have appeared before haven't you?" I told her that although I had, I couldn't remember when. She said, "don't worry, George is coming later, and he will tell you anything you want to know." George was the unofficial archivist of 'Summer Wine', and when he arrived, told me the dates of my previous appearances, and even reminded me of the dialogue I had spoken. This was from the last thirty years – astounding!

Fan mail is often sent to the studios, who then forward it to your agent, and then the agent sends it on. Over the years, I must have received at least a dozen. This works out at approximately one every four years, and I do my level best to reply to this torrent. One was from a chap who was a real fan of 'Summer Wine' and could not get out much. I correspond with him by email and find him to be smashing company even though we have never met.

16: A Vicar Speaks

Being a taxi driver came in useful when I was summoned one day to meet Noel Edmonds. This was at the time he was fronting the *Late Late Breakfast Show*. Every week he used to do a segment where a member of the public would have tricks played upon them.

We were at the Piccadilly Hotel in Manchester, and a cab driver was summoned. An actor called John Judd played a businessman, and I was a 'real' taxi driver who had been running him around. The cabbie, a rough looking man in his mid thirties, came to the hotel room. John asked him how long it would take him to get to the airport. The man said, "about half an hour."

John then said, "right I want you to take me to the bank across the road, wait with your engine running, don't worry if you hear a few bangs, and then rush me straight to the airport." He left the room, leaving his briefcase open, and on the top of a few documents was a gun.

The cabbie said to me "F... me, look a gun." I decided to be a bit obtuse and said that I had been running him around for two days, and he seemed OK. He said "yes, but are you f....ing thick? There's a gun in his briefcase. He's going to rob the bank."

I showed him my genuine taxi badge and said, "don't worry, the gun's probably fake." He exploded," fake, f...ing fake, suppose it's real, what the f... am I going to do?" John came back into the room and the man started shouting, "look mate, I've seen the f...ing gun, and I don't want anything to do with robbing f...ing banks, so you can f...off and get some other f...er to f...ing well do it."

By now, I was getting worried because the man was frighteningly aggressive. It was such a relief to see Noel come in. When he calmed down a bit, the cabbie saw the funny side, and said f... me, I never f...ing thought I would f...ing well fall for a f...ing trick like that." The segment was broadcast the following Saturday, and Noel prefaced the piece by saying that it was the most 'bleeped' item in television history.

Noel Edmonds was a gentleman, and the two days I spent in his company were a delight.

This is the only time my taxi badge was any good, I have been for plenty of parts as a taxi driver over the years, and been unsuccessful. Perhaps I don't look like people's perception of what a cabbie should be?

Down to Granada once again to be auditioned for Corrie. This time for the part of a vicar. Surprise, surprise, I got it and finished up burying Lisa Duckworth, who had been knocked down outside the house she had been living in with Des Barnes. This was a big storyline and Terry Duckworth was to be let out of prison for the funeral.

After turning up at the new Stage One, and being fitted out for surplice and vestments, a fleet of limousines arrived to take us to the location in South Manchester. It was lovely for me to travel in such style and I was in a car, which had an extra seat in the middle. I had Jack Duckworth one side, Des Barnes on the other, whilst behind on the back seat were Vera Duckworth, Terry Duckworth, and Ken Barlow. We stopped at traffic lights on Princess Parkway, and a car stopped next to us. The lady's face was a picture. She looked at us, thought *I know them from somewhere*, and then let out a loud squeal to the friend sat next to her. No one in our car seemed to notice, but I did, and gave them a royal wave. I could imagine her trying to explain to someone, "no honest they were all in the car, but the only wave I got was from this moth-eaten vicar."

The papers were all over the location at Southern Cemetery as the storylines in those days were not leaked and long lens cameras were pointed by men up trees and the graveside had to be covered by screens. I was quite excited as I had plenty of dialogue, but soon realised that while I was speaking, the cameras would be panning around the graveside to catch the reactions of the principals. This became a recurring theme during my Coronation Street appearances, we guest players are never allowed to dominate the action. Quite rightly the camera positions always favoured the regulars, and when you think about it no one would tune in to watch a vicar, postman, taxi driver or policeman. What they want is, Jack, Vera, Terry, Des, and so on.

We had a line run and the director seemed happy enough. We stood down for the lighting people to do their work. Bill Tarmey called me aside and said," are you going to do it like that Jim?" I stuttered "what... I'm not sure... how do you mean Bill? He just said "no, OK, that's fine if that's how you're going to do it," and walked away. The next thirty minutes saw a demented vicar walking around the cemetery mumbling to himself. What was I doing wrong? Bill knew something was not right, and he didn't like to tell me. He took pity on me after a while and came up and said" I was only kidding you know." I had fallen for the oldest actor's trick in the book, to underline someone's uncertainties about their performance and leave them to stew, but it was good-natured, and we all had a chuckle.

One of the interesting developments in this storyline was the reappearance of Nigel Pivaro as Terry Duckworth. He first appeared in the show as a handsome teenager, and for some years had appeared unassailable. I worked in panto with Nigel some time later and as one Salford lad to another, got on pretty well. He never discussed why he was written out, but there is no doubt he felt a sense of regret.

Every time I went down to work on *Coronation Street*, I was in my element. The days of rehearsing on the fifth floor in the main Granada building had long gone. A special building had been built to house the permanent sets, individual dressing rooms for the stars had been built, which seemed to work on a seniority system with the better known 'stars' on the ground level, and the lesser ones over two further floors. This was called Stage One, and housed a luxurious green room where everybody went to relax and socialise. This contained a little kitchen with coffee and tea making facilities, deep leather settees, and everything to make the artists comfortable.

More importantly the techniques of the filming of the programme changed enormously. We would now record each scene individually. This was a lot less pressure in one way but caused problems in another. The actors did not have the sense of the whole picture, and were encapsulated in their individual bubble, and even if they were in the same episode, people might never meet for weeks. The numbers of episodes were gradually increased to the present five a week and entailed an increase in the core cast from around fifteen, to about fifty or so. The storylines were not shot in chronological order and people would never be sure of their continuity, this entailed an army of people to check and make sure that characters were in the right place at the right time. Shooting out of sequence was a particularly difficult skill. One character told me once, that she had shot the funeral scene of her husband in the morning and that same afternoon was filming a light-hearted session with him in the Rovers. Motivation in such circumstances is difficult. In fact, it sometimes seems that the regulars belong to the 'Speak up and don't bump into the furniture,' school of acting. The fact that they make it so realistic under these conditions is greatly to their credit.

Whenever I got a part in 'the street ', I would receive the script at least two weeks in advance. I was very meticulous about learning my lines because I was terrified of holding everything up on the recording day. Every actor I have spoken to over the years has said how nerve-wracking it is to arrive to do a guest spot on a long running series. The people already working there: actors, directors, cameramen, make-up, are part of a well-oiled machine and have worked together in some cases for 20 years or more.

Although every effort is made to make you feel at home, it can be tremendously daunting to suddenly be appearing with people you have been watching for decades on television.

I always arrived hours earlier than my official call time, and would sit in the green room. Every actor when they saw a new face would make a point of coming over, shake hands and introduce themselves. I would wait in the hope that Bill Tarmey, Ann Kirkbride, or Barbara Mullany – now Knox – would come in. They would always have a chat, and this would settle my nerves..

I have been told that each week, pictures of any guest actors appearing for the first time are posted on the green room notice board with a jocular sign underneath saying, 'Be kind to them'. This is perhaps recognition that it is not easy to do your best work when appearing for the first time, especially if your brain wanders to the fact that ten million viewers will watch this.

The regulars wandered around with reams of scripts in different colours to differentiate the episodes. When they finished one scene, they would start to learn the lines for the next. Many actors had difficulty remembering their lines and there are plenty of tales of characters having their words written on beer mats in the Rovers, or on their hands. I'm never surprised when I hear that an actor is leaving after a certain time, as the pressure to perform day after day, is intense.

I only once went up to the *Coronation Street* inner sanctum on the fifth floor of the main building at Granada. What an eye-opener. There was something like ten people just typing and copying scripts in different colours. A script would require sending to 50 or so actors and a further fifty people ranging from executive directors, directors, camera crew, wardrobe, continuity, make-up and props. In a corner, was a series of cubbyholes, which contained little photograph cards of the main cast, which they would sign, and they would be sent to fans that had written in. As there are so many episodes now, it must be a logistical nightmare to get everyone in the right place. There were often two and sometimes three film crews, especially in the run up to Christmas when episodes had to be stockpiled to allow the cast time off.

There were separate offices, of course, for the producer, casting people and important executives. The producer is the overall boss and the actors were never happy to be summoned to his office. I quickly realised that even the relatively well-known characters suffered the same insecurities as the rest of us. What if their contract was not renewed? Were they now typecast, having appeared up to five nights a week in our living rooms? Many had come as youngsters, maybe straight from youth theatre and unlike say, Barbara Knox, had never served an 'apprenticeship'. You can count on one hand the people who have had lasting success after 'The Street.' Everyone was aware of this, but it was a taboo subject, and I never heard it talked about.

Whatever one's personal thoughts about the merits of *Coronation Street*, there is no doubt that it is the most famous and popular programme in the history of British Television, and it is very rarely out of the top ten in the viewers' ratings. It must be said, that six episodes a week is a nearly impossible undertaking. Coming up with new plot-lines that the public will accept is not easy and, on the rare occasions when the standard slips, the tabloids go to town. However, people have grown up with the 'Street' and it has a fan base, which is steadfast and loyal.

Guess what my next job was? Yes, a vicar, but this time in *Hollyoaks*. Over to Mersey TV, and a week on the teen soap. The story this time was a wedding rehearsal at which everything went wrong and the vicar got annoyed, and castigated everyone in sight. It was very enjoyable to do, but I couldn't figure out how they were going to film the wedding, as I had not been booked. I found out when the programme was transmitted. As the vicar in the actual wedding had nothing to say, Mersey TV used an extra to save money. I was told by a member of the cast that they spent twice as long to shoot the wedding scene because they dare not show the vicar's face. Of course, it was false economy, and a humiliating 'slight' for me, but I should have been used to it.

17: An End to the Clubs

By now, I was well into my forties, taxi driving during the day, going to clubs at weekends, and some midweek evenings, and drinking too much. I had always been a good social drinker and could hold my own with anybody. I never drank in clubs because of fear of being breathalysed, and when I arrived home at midnight, couldn't go straight to bed because of the adrenaline still flowing after my performance. Despite the fact that I might have to be up at seven the next morning, I would have a few whiskies to help me sleep. This was also before the time of video and the television would finish about midnight. I would search desperately for something – anything – to watch. I am probably the only person in the world to have seen every single episode of *Bluey,* an Australian programme about a fat, out of condition detective, who puffed and panted his way round Sydney. It was awful, but it was the only thing on, before ITV closed down for the night.

It seemed that *Bluey* was not the only one who was out of condition; I awoke at two in the morning with pains in my chest. I took some indigestion tablets, but it was no good. I woke Helen. She took me straight to Bury General, which was just at the top of our road. The duty nurse was certain that my cardiograph reading showed that I had suffered a heart attack, and I was taken to the Cardiac unit. Now I had plenty of time to think about what was really important. Helen told me that Andrew had told her that he would look after her and would cut the grass.

Three of the longest days of my life followed and I realised that I would have to come to terms with my diagnosis. I had no choice. On the third day, the top heart specialist for the hospital visited me and he expressed doubts. After further exhaustive tests, I was told that it had not been a heart attack and jocularly warned about wasting people's time. I never got to the bottom of what it was. The general consensus was stress, and I went home a very relieved and thankful man.

Helen had very bravely taken a year off from teaching and had taken a degree in 'Special Needs', at Manchester University. Andrew, Lucy and I were immensely proud of her. She taught in 'special' schools for the rest of her career with her usual complete honesty and dedication. How lucky I have been to have met her in that pub that day.

My children continued to keep me on my toes. They were not angels, but we kept them busy with piano lessons (which poor Lucy hated), swimming, Scouts, and Guides and they seemed happy. Lucy was displaying a worrying tendency towards acting and was appearing in the local church panto and school productions.

Our local authority had a strong music service. The children would start as tots in the beginner's groups and, if they stuck at it, eventually finish up in the prestigious 'Bury Youth Orchestra'. Both did progress: Andrew on trombone, and Lucy on Cornet. The final Concert of the year would be the Youth Orchestra, at the Manchester Royal College of Music. This was a very moving performance and would be the last show for a lot of the musicians who would take a bow as leavers. There were tears in a lot of eyes, and when Andrew and Lucy took their leaving bows, at different times, they had been in the Music service for eleven years. The Orchestra also had the side effect of introducing Helen and me to some classical pieces, which we now enjoy.

One night, I was working in a club in Huddersfield. The concert secretary, who was also the compere, told me that there would be an announcement just before my first spot. I thought no more about it and on he went. "Ladies and gentlemen, I'm afraid that I have some very bad news. Harry, the longest serving member of our club died last night, and I would like you all to stand while the organist plays 'Abide with me'. The organist played and there was not a dry eye in the house, and with an audience full of tears he announced, "Here's your comedian Jim Whelan."

Only a week later, this time in Oldham, Helen came with me. Before my first spot, the concert secretary after saying hello said, "Just before you go on Jim, I've got an announcement to make."

"No-one dead I hope?" I said.

"Yes, how did you know?" He replied.

"Look, I know it's very sad, but if you make the announcement before I go on, it will kill the atmosphere and spoil everyone's night, could you do it after my first spot?" He called a committee meeting there and then, and after half an hour of deep discussion came back and said that I had won, and they would do it later after my spot, but told me in no uncertain terms that this was the first time since the club had opened, that this had happened.

As an established club 'turn', I had learned to handle an audience, especially hecklers. To be fair, it didn't happen very often, but when it did, you had to verbally jump on them otherwise, you were lost. Consequently, I armed myself with a few tried and trusted 'put downs', and as I had a mike and they didn't, I was usually the winner. One of my favourites was, "I'll tell you what pal, and God ruined a good arse when he put teeth in your mouth." This got me many belly laughs. The audience were amazed at my quick-fire repartee, but I didn't always come out on top. Witness the following exchange in Liverpool:

Me: finishing a story that had died.

Heckler: "Call that a joke?"

Me: "Aye aye, you barracked me ten years ago didn't you?"

Heckler: "Yes, I did."

Me: "I remember your bloody shirt."

Heckler: "I remember your fuckin' jokes."

Nights like these amused me rather than making me upset, but as I was now in my fifties, I knew that I could not continue to travel up and down the country working in clubs. I decided to retire from the treadmill of being a club 'turn'.

What had started 30 years earlier as a ruse to get my Equity card had provided me with a living. Not to mention a host of memories. What sticks in my mind as I look back from a distance is, in those 30 years never once was I ever conned or cheated out of money by a working man. Never was I made to feel inadequate or second rate, and although many times my comedy did not appeal to every club, I was always given a chance. I have nothing but respect and affection for the working men's clubs of this country and greatly regret that they are closing in the present climate.

18: Square Deal Shoes

Taxi driving was getting me down and I decided that I would open a shop.

My neighbour had a highly successful market stall selling shoes and with his advice and a bank loan, I opened up in Prestwich. For the first few years, I used to work at the shop during the day and still do the clubs at weekends. I cannot really imagine how I did it now, but I kept going I suppose, through a mixture of relative youth and adrenaline. The best day at the shop was of course Saturdays. The shop was managed by my sister-in-law, 'Trish', who married my youngest brother Billy. We would have plenty of customers all day. I would go home, have a bath, and head out to a club somewhere. The nerves that I still felt before going on stage helped me through the evening, but going home at midnight, I could barely keep my eyes open. As far as the act was concerned, I was on autopilot, nothing ever changed, and I had to make sure that I didn't appear at the same clubs too often, as they would remember my jokes. Still, I was going down pretty well at most venues, and I had no trouble getting bookings.

Trish's husband – my brother Billy – had two boys who were good footballers and he helped to run the local teams. Liam particularly was very promising and played in the town team Salford Boys. I asked Trish one day who they were playing.

"Saint Helens Town. The best team in the north," she said.

"Do you think we've got any chance?" I asked her.

"We might have if Wilson is playing."

Ryan Wilson was someone who Liam had kept out of the team for a short time, because of his greater physique, but even as an undersized kid, Wilson could not be kept out for long. After his mum and dad split, Ryan took his Mum's name and went on to slightly better things. His Mum's maiden name was Giggs.

Andrew used to come to the shop on a Saturday to help out. There was always time-consuming things to do like lacing up trainers. Trish and I used to lay bets on how long he would last before asking, "Dad can I go and get a bacon butty from the café?"

We built up trade by selling absolutely every kind of footwear. Men's shoes, trainers, wellies, work boots and slippers. Ladies court shoes, fashion boots, children's school shoes, pumps, ladies and children's wellies and trainers, canvas shoes in the summer and anything else we could think of. Lots of our customers became our friends, and we watched young children growing up and graduating from our shoes to fashion footwear as they got older.

Although never at the cutting edge where technology was concerned, I bought a cordless phone and set it up at the shop. It may seem archaic now, but to be able to walk about and speak on the phone was a great advantage in those days, especially as the calls cost no more than usual. Unlike these new-fangled mobile things, which were just beginning to appear, but were prohibitively expensive.

Everybody loved Trish, who ran the shop while I went buying stock, or was off doing my telly or theatre bits. An old lady used to come in nearly every day, just to have a chat to her. One day this lady came in while Trish was on the phone.

"Ooh Trish, I love your phone, are they expensive to use?"

Trish said: "No they're the same as ordinary calls once it's set up."

"Ooh, mine's in the draught in my hall and by the time I get there, I miss lots of calls. Please will you get me one? I'll gladly give you the money."

We got a phone and base set and fitted it up for her in the house. Two days later, she came in with everything in a polythene bag. "Trish, I don't want this phone, it's no good." When we gently enquired why not, she said, "I've been trying to phone my lad from Tesco's, and nothing happens."

Next door to the shop was the Grapes pub, and the landlord was a very pleasant chap called Dave. He was a good businessman and had two terrific looking daughters. The youngest, called Jenny, used to come into the shop a lot and came in once looking really downcast. When Trish asked her what was wrong, she said that she had been to audition for some modelling work and had been turned down. We tried to cheer her up but without much success and off she went. Some years later her dreams came true and she auditioned – this time successfully – for 'Atomic Kitten'. Jenny Frost. She always was a lovely girl, and I doubt that she has changed.

In the same class as me at St Thomas of Canterbury School, was a boy called John Ruane. John quickly grew bigger than the rest of us and because of his size. He was the goalkeeper for the school football team. As we lived in the same street, we still saw each other when I went to grammar school, and when we were about fifteen years old, I became aware of his younger brother Martin. Martin was four years younger than us, but even though he was only eleven, was bigger than John, never mind the rest of us.

I next met him ten years later in a rough pub near the docks on Cross Lane, which was known locally as the 'Barbary Coast'. He was friendly enough, and we shared a few pints, but he seemed on edge. I soon found out why. Because of his size, he was now about six foot eight, and twenty-nine stone. He was always being challenged by any local 'hard man' who wanted to build a reputation. Sure enough, a yobbo came up and started insulting him. Martin told the man that all he wanted was a quiet drink and to be left alone, but the man kept on and on, until Martin, goaded beyond endurance wiped the floor with him, leaving him in a crumpled heap.

It was a further ten years when a big American left-hand drive car pulled up outside the shop and blew its horn. I went out and it was Martin who was driving this monster, the steering wheel like a polo mint in his enormous hands. He said, "I was told you'd opened a shoe shop, and I wanted you to get me half a dozen pairs of expensive trainers." I asked him what size and he said, "17 or 18," and then collapsed laughing.

He was now called Giant Haystacks, and had made a terrific impact in the wrestling world, but in the conversations I had with him over the next couple of years, he never seemed happy. I asked him if he wanted to go for a pint, but he said that he wouldn't because the aggravation was worse than ever now that he was famous. People just would not leave him alone.

He died tragically young. I always got the impression that Martin just wanted to be an ordinary family man, left alone to make his way in the world, but because of circumstances, was forced into a celebrity persona, which was never what he was really like.

I kept the shop for some fifteen years and until the great depression in the late '90s, traded quite successfully. The arrival of Tesco, and the advent of Sunday trading, spelled doom for small traders, and reluctantly, I closed.

19: Return to Contact

Like a lot of actors, I was absolutely hopeless at accounts. If anyone showed me a spreadsheet, I would go dizzy, so I needed an accountant. I had met Mike Little socially and become quite friendly with him and he took over my affairs.

Mike and Eileen (Mike's wife), were both accountants and, over the years, I have been looked after by firstly Mike, and when he split up with her, by Eileen. They had mentioned their son now and again, and in fact Eileen had brought him to see me in panto in Rochdale. Although he was a very clever boy and was at the Bolton School locally, he harboured thoughts that he might become an actor. He had joined the locally run Carol Godby acting school, which Carol also ran as an agency for young actors.

He soon obtained some TV parts and was engaged to play a patient in Granada's *Children's Ward*. While he was rehearsing one day, Caroline Aherne was talking on the fifth floor to June West, who was casting for a new programme that Granada was making for the BBC. Caroline had cast the complete show but couldn't find anyone to play the put upon young son. She looked on the monitor which all the casting people had in their offices to check on programmes, and said to June West, "that's just the boy we need." June said she would get him in for an audition, but Caroline said, "We don't need an audition. He is just what we want." The young man in the right place at the right time was Ralf Little. The programme that Caroline was referring to, *The Royle Family*.

David Williams phoned me one morning to tell me that he had been approached by Noreen Kershaw to play a part in *Llysistrata* at the Contact Theatre. Noreen was a fine actress, who was also achieving success as a television and theatre director. He was not available, but told Noreen that I would fit the bill. Although I had met Noreen socially, she felt that I was too inexperienced in 'serious' theatre work to be considered. I thanked David and thought no more about it. Three weeks later, Noreen rang and asked if I would still be interested. Reading between the lines, I was probably sixth choice for the part, but I was not proud and readily accepted.

So, after a mere 20 years or so, I was making my return to the scene of my first professional theatre appearance. 'A really enjoyable experience' is how I described it to someone, and it was interesting that the nerves were still in evidence. On the opening night, whilst waiting for the curtain to open, my knees were literally knocking and my legs trembling. A very experienced actress called Val Lilley, who saw my fright and gently, but surely, helped me through it, played my wife in the production.

I bonded to some extent on this job with a local actor who, like me, was doing the rounds of auditions and, again like me, playing small peripheral parts. I kept an eye on him over the years and always thought that he gave extremely truthful performances. His persistence was rewarded last year when Ken Loach recognised his talent and cast him as the lead in his film *Looking for Eric*. He played Eric the postman opposite the 'other' Eric, Mr Cantona, and gave a terrific performance. His name was Steve Evets.

The fact that I knew Noreen slightly socially, made me think that I might have an easy time. I could not be more wrong. One day during rehearsals when she could not get the level of performance that she wanted from me, she made me stay behind and locked the door. "You're not leaving this room until you give me a 'theatre' performance." I had fallen into the trap of 'telly' acting, lowering my voice too much, making my gestures and movements much too small. This was unacceptable. Noreen knew this and put me through hell until I came up to her expectations. We opened to reasonable notices, and if things go according to plan, I should be back there round about 2020. Perhaps in view of the Pandemic, it's as well that I wasn't scheduled to reappear.

When the production finished, I wondered what to do. My children were growing up and Andrew was in his final year at Holy Cross Sixth Form College in Bury. He said one day that he would like to try to become a doctor. We were never sure where this impulse came from. He was a normal teenager, a decent musician and good at maths. We hoped that it was not just a temporary inclination, as we knew that medical school was difficult and obviously there was no history of medicine, or indeed of any higher education, from my side of the family. Perhaps he was being a little ambitious?

Unlike what happened with my dad, Helen and I told him that we would support him in every way possible. He applied to several Medical Schools and was eventually accepted by Sheffield University.

I now had a dilemma. Andrew was embarking on what would be five years of training, and we had pledged to support him. I had no visible means of support. Television and theatre jobs were in short supply, so what to do?

I started taxi driving again. I had no choice. Andrew had to be supported, and the treadmill restarted, with a difference. I found that things had changed drastically while I had been away. There were a lot more taxis on the road as more people became redundant. For a while I felt really low and worthless, especially as I was starting driving at four in the morning. At this hour, the night drivers had gone home after the nightclub rush at 2.00am, and the majority of day drivers didn't start till seven. This meant that we early birds could earn good money for these hours. I hated the winter mornings when I had to scrape the frost from my car. I would feel as if I was the only person up at that time and it always reminded me of my paper round as a kid.

As I had lived in the Higher Broughton area of Salford, it made sense for me to do a lot of my taxiing there. Knowing the district was an advantage, but it had another plus point for me. The area around Broughton Park was mainly a Jewish enclave and a lot of work came from the Orthodox community. In the main, we would take the 'froomers' for hospital appointments, shopping, or to the station and, maybe because I had lived with Jewish people all of my life, I got on reasonably well with them. It had to be said though, their continuous demands used to drive us mad. A typical exchange, for instance, would be on one of my early mornings. Mr Rosenberg had booked a car the night before to take him to the airport at 5.00am. At 4.55am, he would phone the controller to make sure the taxi was on its way. At 5.00am, I would knock on the door. At 5.05am the door would open on the chain and a voice would ask:" Yes who is it?" As there was a man with a Salford City taxi driver badge standing at the door and a car with its engine running with a giant Blueline sign on it, and as he had booked a taxi to take him to the airport, you would think that this would be a clue, but not so.

"Taxi," I would say.

"Who for?" would come the reply.

"You," I would say, becoming exasperated. The door would shut, and he would come out ten minutes later. He had booked it early in case we were late.

Looking back, this seems so trivial, but when it happened time and time again the effect was to alienate our drivers. Blueline taxis had around one hundred cars on the road, and eighty of them would not go near Broughton Park because they could not stand it. However, there was never any doubt about getting paid from the 'community' people. No driver ever had 'run offs', and I made quite a few acquaintances on my rounds. You could never say 'friends', because the cultural differences made this impossible, but a sense of humour certainly helped you through a shift.

We used to have arguments all of the time with certain regulars. One was the headmaster of the local Jewish school, and he had a regular booking each day at 8.25am. Not 8.24, he would not come out. If it got to 8.26, he would be on the phone to the controller. He only went round the corner to his school and nobody wanted to do such a crappy job, because the traffic on his route was horrible. The problem all taxi drivers faced with jobs like this was, they would be waiting at 8.00am and a call would come through to take someone into the city. By taking this fare, it meant that we would be late for our headmaster, but our choice was to earn £5 for the town job, or wait twenty-five minutes and get 90 pence. After suffering a tirade one morning, I asked him why he didn't use another taxi firm and he replied that no one else would have him.

I had never driven taxis at night. The night drivers were a different breed. They had to deal with the drunks, or 'runners' who didn't want to pay. Some were mugged for their takings. Most of my early morning jobs were people on the early shift, nurses and such, who did not have cars and as there wouldn't be any buses, they used cabs. The day shifts were much safer.

Some of the night driver's stories used to give me the willies. One favourite trick was for a person to phone a cab to take them around various pubs for two or three hours. When the cab turned up, three or four men got in and ordered the car to take them around, leaving one man in the car to see that the driver didn't scarper, and then they wouldn't pay him at the end of the night. This became known as the drug run, for obvious reasons, and often the driver would be robbed of his takings as well. Of course, the controller would refuse this job if he could, but often, he had no way of knowing in advance.

My taxi driving used to include the Salford area. Very often, after I had dropped a fare in 'town', I would wait at the United training ground at the Cliff for my next job to come over the radio. They used to open the gates at six, and I used to have a chat to the early morning cleaners, or the chefs when they came out for a fag. Alex Ferguson always came in shortly after seven, and he would always say hello. He has many detractors for his abrasive style, but this was never in evidence on the occasions I saw him. The people on the staff from the cleaners upwards were always treated as if they were tremendously important, and you would never hear a bad word about him from any of the 'ordinary' workers.

When Helen and I went to the 50th wedding anniversary of an old Irish uncle of mine, an equally old Irish aunt cornered me at the bar. "They tell me your son is at University?" She said.

"Yes Auntie."

"He's doing medicine?" I nodded. "When he's finished, he'll be a nurse?"

"No Auntie, if he passes his exams, he will be a doctor."

"Arrah, he won't, you're deluded," she said, and walked away in disgust. This gives some sort of insight into the mind-set of the Irish community in which I was brought up. Why did I have to leave De La Salle? Why wasn't I allowed to become a journalist? I was now in my mid 50s with no money, no prospects and a drink problem, which would have to be addressed.

A call from Noreen Kershaw, who directed me at Contact theatre, came next. She knew about my cabaret experience and asked if I would act as compere in a charity show for a Bury based charity for children with special needs. The show was to star a writer and performer who used to be a teacher in Yorkshire, his name Gervase Phynn. The lady who was running the show told me that she wrote to Gervase to ask how much he would consider charging to come and appear for the charity. Gervase replied instantly and, after making a few enquiries about the charity, said that he would do the show for nothing. On the night of the show, he came all the way from Doncaster in terrible weather and gave a magnificent performance. What a funny man. Proof if any were needed, that good and generous people do exist.

20: Brookside

I was desperate to try to resuscitate my floundering acting career. I applied and was taken on as an actor by a co-op agency. Inter City Casting was one of the first actors' co-ops in Manchester. The theory behind it was the actors would run the office themselves, trying to drum up work for each other, and the actors would each do three or so days each month as admin in the office if they were available.

It was good for me in that I could get an idea of how the process of being an agent worked and made friends with the thirty or so actors on our books. Every month, we had a meeting of all the members who were available and, at one of the first meetings, I came across a young actor who was filming a new series. We asked how it was going, and he told us that it was the worst job he had ever done. The actors were arguing amongst themselves, the directors didn't seem to know what they were doing, and the powers that be were going to 'bury' it to save everyone's embarrassment. The actor was Mark Jordon. The programme was *Heartbeat*, and the rest is history. It just goes to show how no one really knows what the public wants.

My mate from Oldham Rep, David Williams, was with the co-op and we used to contrive to work together in the office. One day he brought in a letter from British actors' Equity informing him that a young actor just starting out had requested that he could use the name David Williams. As only one actor could have a name, he was refused and had taken another name. David and I had a quiet chuckle, who would ever get anywhere in the business with a name like David Walliams?

As I got my feet under the table at Inter City, I realised a few things that most people never did. The ratio of auditions to jobs was on average, seven to one. This means that an actor would go to seven interviews before getting a job and as most actors got about five interviews a year, the odds against, were daunting. The things that hurt the most were the near misses. We had an incredibly talented actress on our books called Christine Parle. She was called to audition for a regular part in *Emmerdale*. When you are up for a regular in a long running series, the process can be laborious. The girl had three separate interviews and was down to the last two. She then had to undergo a screen test and wait a further two weeks for a final decision. I was in the office when the call came from Yorkshire to say that she was unsuccessful and had to ring her to tell her. Her mum answered the phone and I told her the bad news as gently as I could. She was in tears for her poor daughter, who had lived in hope for so many weeks, and I felt rotten. What a miserable, cruel, harsh business.

Another dispiriting chapter was for the young Chris Bisson. Chris was a very handsome young man, and we in the agency, thought he could do well. One of his first auditions was for a drinks advert, which would entail a large fee, generous repeats, and three days filming in Hong Kong. To everyone's excitement, Chris was chosen, and he readied himself for his trip. The day before he was due to travel, the clients discovered that he was only 17 years old. Although it had not been stipulated that he should be 18, He was below the legal age for alcohol consumption and he lost the job. Although he was philosophical about it, he was very despondent. Chris had no need to worry. He was soon snapped up by Granada and spent a few years as Vikram in *Coronation Street*. There was always more to Chris than just wanting to stay in Corrie, and he left, turned up in *I'm a Celebrity, Get Me Out of Here*, appeared as a regular in *Shameless,* and is at present a regular on *Emmerdale*.

In the Agency, we had a venerable actor named Anthony Benson. Tony was from the old school and had spent many years in repertory theatre. He used to smoke like a chimney and maintained that it was too late for him to stop, despite his chest rattling every time he spoke. One day, a call came in for him to play a Clerk of the Court in a big upcoming storyline in *Brookside*. He did the first day and took ill, being rushed to Hospital with chest problems. Mersey Television were in a panic and after some discussion, I was dispatched.

My first lines were to Anna Friel, who was charged with the murder of her father. I settled in for a nine-day shoot. A special courtroom studio had been built in the Merseyside complex to accommodate this storyline. The prosecuting counsel was Philip Madoc, a superb actor. I was sitting close to him for the whole of the 'trial '. For me, it was a master class in acting, Philip had been at the top of the profession for a long time, and I watched with complete admiration. I have never kidded myself that I was anything special compared to such performers, but at least on this job, I had time to look and learn. The courtroom was small and claustrophobic and every day there were upwards of fifty people there. Four cameras, court officials, extras playing pressmen and members of the public, make-up, wardrobe and technicians squashed in. Our nine-day shoot covered the full 'body under the patio' trial, and bits from the trial were inserted into six episodes of *Brookside*. This was great for small timers like me, as we were paid for six episodes. Without doubt, the happiest memory of this job was my first meeting with Mike Starke, who played Sinbad. He is the funniest person I have ever met and made us laugh so much during the tense scenes, that he was eventually banned from the set except when he was in shot.

My main work was at the end of the nine days when the verdicts were announced. I had tons of dialogue. We shot two different outcomes, so the results could not be leaked, and press speculation led to frenzy as transmission approached. On the night the episode aired, Brookside was watched by almost ten million viewers. The biggest audience figures in their history. It became a sort of 'iconic' moment in British TV.

Tony Benson died shortly afterwards, and my enjoyment of the job was tempered when I remembered that I had only got it through the misfortune of someone who I liked and admired. Although I realised that it was not my fault, it still it made me realise yet again, how precarious and cruel this business could be and how precious life is.

On the same Brookside job, I met a man who is one of the unsung heroes of television production. The first assistant director, sometimes known as the floor manager, is the all-important link between the director up in his gallery, and the actors. His job is to pass directions on to us, and generally keep things under control. The *Brookside* first AD was John Folkard. He was a genuinely nice, funny, but firm man, and had us all in stitches whilst never letting us get out of hand. Actors are like kids in a lot of ways and sometimes need firm, but always tactful, handling. John is a master of his craft and I was to meet him again when he moved to *Coronation Street*.

21: Martin Clunes & Jeremy Brett

An interesting trip to Yorkshire Television came next. I was to play a small part in a thriller called *Chiller*. My scene was as a mortuary attendant, and the play starred a little known actor called Martin Clunes. Having gone through my usual wardrobe checks and make-up at the main studios, I was ushered to a waiting car that was to take me to the hospital where the mortuary filming was taking place, stopping to pick up Martin from his hotel on the way. He was very pleasant, and we had a chat whilst sharing a Winnebago at the location.

I had arranged to call Helen sometime during the day, but as we were in hospital grounds, I couldn't find a phone box anywhere. Martin delved into his briefcase and brought out something a bit bigger than a house brick. "There you go Jim, why don't you ring her on my mobile phone?" I had heard of these things, but had never seen one before, and Martin showed me how to use it. I thought it was wonderful, but I was sure that they would never catch on. Who could afford to carry their own personal telephone around with them? It was ludicrous.

Apart from my first sight of a mobile, my only memories of that day were of a pleasant shoot. Martin mentioned in passing that he was hoping to start on a new series soon, something to do with two bachelors sharing a flat and behaving not so well, best of luck with that mate.

Staying in Yorkshire, I made the first of about six appearances in *Heartbeat*. It was nice to meet up again with Mark Jordon, who had settled nicely into the character of 'PC Bellamy', and was to stay for 14 series in what he came to call, his 'golden handcuffs'. This was the problem when one landed a part in a high-profile series, were you now typecast? Would you ever get to play anything else? Is this it? For some of us, this would be a wonderful problem to have and, to be fair, Mark was a consummate professional, and made the part memorably believable. My involvement over the years was particularly unmemorable, but I always enjoyed my trips to 'Aidenfield'.

One upside of being in a co-op was that we all tried to help one another. We had an actor in Rep at Oldham, and whilst chatting to a fellow member of the cast, he asked him what he was doing next. The chap said that he was directing the upcoming panto in Lancaster and had cast everybody except Baron Hardup. The actor told him how wonderful I was, and I was offered the part.

I hadn't done panto since Oldham, and wasn't at all sure if I could still cut it so I decided to wait a day and ask Helen and the kids. Helen was not too sure, but the kids absolutely insisted that I do it. I think they were 'taking the mick'. I took the part, and it was as if the intervening years since Oldham had never happened. I loved it and had a great time. I also did Panto the following year.

Working in Lancaster meant awfully long days. I would get up at seven thirty, drop the children off at school at eight thirty, and open the shop at nine. Trish would come in at eleven, and I travelled to the Dukes theatre for the matinee. Between shows, I would try to rest in the dressing room, do the evening show, and get home by maybe, midnight.

An actor called Paul Oldham played the 'baddie'. His claim to fame was that he had played a young 'compo', in a series called *First of the Summer Wine*. Paul was a smashing panto performer and, as he lived in Manchester, he came to the shop and we commuted together. Looking back, it might have been better to stay in digs near the theatre, but as I had to run the shop with Trish, this was not possible. Paul was good company, and kept me awake on the homeward journeys.

A side effect of this show was that Lucy also wanted to come with me every single day. I was very gratified and pleased that she wanted to be with her old Dad all the time, but I soon realised that she was in love with theatre. Special permission was sought for her to sit backstage and watch all the shows during her school holidays and she became a popular 'member' of the company.

Two years later, I was in panto at the Gracie Fields Theatre in Rochdale. We were doing *Cinderella*, and using a real little pony for the transformation scene. To Lucy's delight, she was appointed the ostler and had to handle the little pony for the full run. She also played the ghost in the traditional haunting scene, where the characters had to be frightened off the stage. A friend brought her five-year-old daughter to the show. On the way home this little girl said to her mum: "Are you sure that was Lucy under the sheet as the ghost?"

"Yes darling."

"And did Jim know that it was her?"

"Of course he did."

"Then why did he run off frightened?"

There's no answer to that.

A lovely job on *Sherlock Holmes* came next, with Jeremy Brett. Brett was quite a famous actor who apparently 'lost' ten or fifteen years of his career to drink. Upon coming to his senses, he was cast as 'Sherlock', and made the part his own. My scene with Jeremy was as the old caretaker who had witnessed a murder and was being quizzed by Holmes. I was a little apprehensive as usual, but I needn't have worried. When we first met Jeremy, he shook my hand, professed that he was glad to meet me, and launched into the following.

"Now look my dear chap, I think that we can have a little fun with your main speech. I would like you to say half of your speech and pause for five seconds, which will give me time to look reflectively out of the window." He left me in no doubt that this is what he wanted. I did not know what to say, so I said nothing and just did as he asked. Of course, it seemed a touch pedantic but as he was the main man, he had to be obeyed. When the programme was transmitted, I knew exactly what he meant. The caretaker said half of his speech, and Holmes' 'look' out of the window told the watching millions that he knew who the murderer was. Sheer genius in a single glance. To this day, I do not know how he did it. It was the alchemy of great acting.

22: AA

My drinking had escalated. The couple of whiskies to help me sleep after coming home from a club had become half a bottle or more a night. I never drank during the day, and I wouldn't touch a drop until I had brought the kids home from swimming, Scouts, orchestra or whatever. Nonetheless, once I started, I found it impossible to stop and although no one seemed to notice, I knew deep inside that I was in trouble.

One day I came across a pamphlet. It said, 'if you are worried about your drinking, try this simple test'. There were 20 questions to answer, such as, 'Do you have blackouts after drink? Do you drink every day'?

I answered yes to only about seven of these questions and was confident that I was OK. When I turned over it said, 'If you have answered yes to two or more, you are an alcoholic'. This was a crash of doom, but deep inside, I knew it was right.

The realisation that I was an alcoholic was an absolute nightmare. I had been drinking since I was fifteen in any Salford pub that would serve me, and there were a few. The men in my family were hard drinking Irishmen and the standing of a man was how he could hold his liquor. I could see no way forward without the crutch of alcohol and one day in desperation, I phoned the help line for Alcoholics Anonymous. The man on the other end of the phone was really understanding, but told me in no uncertain terms that no one could stop me drinking but myself. I tried to convince him that I would only drink at weekends or that I would just drink beer and not spirits, but he was a recovering alcoholic himself and said that he had heard it all before. He left me with a list of AA meetings and told me that if I really wanted to, I could stop.

I took myself to Radcliffe near my home in Bury on a wet, cold Thursday night. I hung around outside the door of the room. I could hear voices, but was afraid to go in. A man came up the steps and said, "Hello I'm Paul, do you want to come in? I said I wasn't sure, and he asked me, "Why don't you just come and have a cup of tea with us, if you don't like it you can leave when you want."

I had always envisaged alcoholics as tramps and lowlifes, drinking white lightning and bottles of cheap sherry, but as I got to know AA, I realised there were all sorts of people, including doctors and professional people who suffered from the disease. Once, I even went to a meeting that was run by a Priest. As the meeting started, Paul said that there was a new person with us this evening and asked me to say my first name. The meeting instantly became all about me, as this was my first visit. People told me their stories and the realisation hit me that I was not alone. Horror stories abounded, of men and women who had lost everything through alcohol. Homes, families and jobs had gone, and it was brought home to me that drink was no respecter of class or social standing. The consensus was that I was lucky that I had realised my alcoholism whilst there was still time. If I continued my present path, what lay ahead for me was almost certain ruin. My relationship with Helen and my children would deteriorate, ill health would follow, and my rock bottom might take many unhappy years to arrive.

This made me think seriously. I could not imagine a future without a drink in my hand. Although I never missed work because of it, I had the most horrendous hangovers and my body had built up a tolerance to alcohol. Just going to a pub for a couple of beers was not enough anymore, I needed some spirits before I could go to bed. When I counted, I had not gone a single night without drink for many years. A fool could see that this could not continue. I saw people who had been in my position, and now were on the mend, they tried to convince me that it was my only option. They were right. There was no way I could just drink like a normal person. I had to face it; I was an alcoholic.

While not pretending that it would be easy, I promised to try to give up. The first few weeks were horrible. I couldn't sleep. I was full of nameless fears in the night and, without the help and support of people who were strangers to me, I would have given in. What kept me going was the realisation of what I had to lose. I had a lovely, supportive wife, Lucy, was by now doing well at Holy Cross College and Andrew was studying hard at Sheffield School of Medicine.

Gradually things got easier and the first night that I slept through the night without booze was a real milestone.

I continued to go to AA meetings for almost two years and I am convinced that alcoholism is a disease. I am eternally grateful to AA. It might not be everyone's cup of tea, but it did the trick for me.

My drinking memories were not all bad. For many years alcohol and I, were the best of friends. A few snifters would help to overcome my shyness, make me feel as if I was as good as the next bloke and it gave me confidence. If I could see a way of just drinking a couple of pints at night, having a glass or two of wine with a meal, that would be fine, but I knew deep down inside, that for me it wasn't an option. With any luck, I will never drink again.

23: Christian Bale & Ray Winstone

The call came one day to do some video recording at the agency and send the results to London. They were casting a feature film by a so-called famous director and were looking to cast some of the smaller parts without the bother of sending a team to Manchester. We got some old *Brookside* scripts and acted out the parts that we thought they would need and sent them off. Three weeks later I received a letter inviting me to play the small part of the father of an unknown actor named Christian Bale. The script would follow. When it came, I was disappointed to find that all my lines were off screen, but as the daily rate was £450, I accepted gratefully.

My filming day was at Bray studios near Windsor. When I arrived, I was taken to a caravan with my name on it and then ignored for 12 hours. Without doubt, I was the most unimportant person in the whole world, and I was ignored again for a second day and asked to go back to my boarding house and return in the morning. On the third day, someone came and told me that they were running a little late and asked if I could come back for a fourth day. My one-day's filming had turned into four, and as far as I was concerned, they could keep this up as long as they liked as I was on – what was to me – a very handsome daily fee.

Finally, I was taken to the giant studio and was introduced to a small tired looking man. He said his name was Todd Haynes and apologised for keeping me waiting so long. We were asked to run through our scene which was one where I, as Christian's dad, had to throw him out of the house when I realised that he was gay. I delivered my lines from off screen and came into shot to manhandle him. Todd liked what he saw and re-jigged the whole scene to accommodate my lines on screen. Suddenly everyone's attitude towards me changed, we shot the scenes from various angles, and even Christian Bale was quite complimentary. When we finished, Todd Haynes put his hand around my shoulder and told me that he was really pleased with my efforts. When

I found out how famous he really was, that meant a lot to me. The film was *Velvet Goldmine* and was well received without becoming a great hit. Ewan McGregor, Eddie Izzard and Toni Colette starred in it. The film was set in the 'Glam Rock' era, but was let down by David Bowie withdrawing permission for his songs to be used. He never told me why.

My next bit of excitement turned out to be the best experience so far of my career. I went to a casting in Manchester for a small but important part in an upcoming feature film. The part I was up for was that of a blind man. When I went in to meet the director, I had no idea what I would do or say. The director asked me how I envisaged the blind man. At first, I was floundering but then I had a brainwave.

Over the years, a midweek regular cabaret venue was a big hotel in Reddish near Stockport called the Pomona. A retired variety artiste who loved live shows ran it, and as midweek bookings were prized, the acts worked it regularly. The pianist was Ricky Raynor, a terrific player who was blind. When we did our 'dots' as the music was called with him, he had a little portable Braille machine on which he tapped something out and put it in the music stand on his piano. Whatever it was worked, because he played like a dream.

What fascinated me about him were his eyes. Although completely blind, his pupils would appear to be looking into the distance, as if he had something else on his mind.

I tried to explain this to David Hay the director. He seemed interested in my interpretation, and I read the part. When I had finished, David left the room and came back in with a woman who I found out later was the producer. I read it again for her and then read a further three times, trying to give a different slant each time. David thanked me for coming and said he would let me know.

Although I knew that I had done well, the following week was still the usual extremes of optimism and despair, but this time with a happy conclusion, I got the part.

Two months later I turned up to my first day's filming at Maine Road, Manchester City's football ground. The film was about a 15-year-old who was bullied at school but was given some 'magic' football boots that helped him and his school team to reach their cup final.

Being greeted by a runner, I was directed to my caravan. When I got to it, I thought there must be some mistake, the paper sign on the door said Ray Winstone in large letters, and mine underneath in much smaller writing. I tentatively knocked on the door, Ray opened it and said, "you must be Jim, come in and I'll get us a cup of tea." I spent the next ten days sharing that caravan with Ray. We quickly found out that we were football supporters and seemed to spend most of the time arguing the merits of West Ham versus Man United.

My scenes as the blind programme seller who turns out to be the first owner of the 'magic' boots were pretty intense, especially the one where he found out that his mother who bought them for him many years ago, before he lost his sight, had died. As this one approached, I became agitated. My nerves at having to play an emotional scene with Ray, in which he had one line and I had all the others, meant I could not sleep the night before. I spent the whole night going over my lines again and again.

We started to rehearse the scene, which ended with the blind man in tears. When John the director had given me some instructions, we went for the first 'take '. Perhaps I was trembling a bit because I felt a hand on my arm giving me a firm squeeze. We got through the first take and for the rest of the day, as is the way with film, it was shot from all angles. Every time John said, "cut", my character was in tears, and every time there was the same pressure on my arm. Nothing was ever said, but the generosity of Ray's little gesture to a completely unknown small-time actor is something that I will always remember. We hear stories in the business of famous actors who have stand-ins to shoot their 'reverses', which are when they are not in shot and the focus is on the lesser characters. This was never even considered by Ray, who endured ten hours in a cold and uncomfortable situation. The difference to me of having him there for the whole time was immense and led I think, to my best performance on film.

One morning Ray and I were having our usual heated discussion on the respective merits of West Ham versus Man United when there was a tap at the door. Thinking it was the runner calling us to the set, I answered it. Outside, there was a giant limousine and a chauffeur in full livery.

"I've come to take you to the location Sir."

"But we're already at the location," I said.

"We just have to walk to the other side of the pitch."

"My instructions are to take you there, sir."

I looked at Ray, who wasn't fazed in the slightest and said, "Just play the game son." We got into the car and to the amusement of everybody else, drove out of the car park, round to the front of the ground, decamped at the main door and walked up to the camera location. I never found out why the car had been booked, and it was not discussed again.

The film was, There's Only One Jimmy Grimble,' and was released six months later. It had a good cast including Ray Winstone, Robert Carlyle,

Gina McKee and a host of northern character actors. We all thought that we had a pretty good film, but two things conspired against it. Number one was that the machinations of the film industry meant that it only received a limited release. I do not understand the politics, but this was apparently a big blow, but not as big as the second.

Billy Elliot was released at the same time rightly to tremendous acclaim. Several reviewers compared us unfavourably, and the film 'died' at the box office.

Some weeks after the release, I was at Yorkshire TV to read for a tiny part in *Emmerdale*. The casting lady, in time-honoured fashion, asked, "what have you been up to Jim?"

I said, "I'm in a new film that's just been released, *Jimmy Grimble*."

"Oh, that's my favourite film, and you were great in it. In fact, I'm going to see it again tomorrow," she said.

At last I thought, someone has seen it, but then she added, "mind you I love ballet dancing."

Perhaps we actors on the lower rungs of the ladder should be used to this kind of ignorance from the people responsible for giving us work. My dilemma was whether to point out her mistake. I took the cowards' route and said nothing. I didn't get the job either.

One happy thing happened during *Jimmy Grimble*. The juvenile lead was played by a very pretty young actress named Samia Ghadi and, although we never met during filming as our paths didn't cross, she made a point of coming up after the premiere and told me that she loved the way the blind man was portrayed and how did I do that 'thing' with my eyes. She of course, has gone on to great success as Maria in *Coronation Street*. We often chat about the making of the film.

24: Lucy & the Braithwaites

At my end of the acting market, I always had to audition. It was soul destroying at times but what was the alternative? If you refused to go to say, London, there were plenty of people who would, even when you always had to pay your own expenses. Many a time when you turned up at a casting session your heart sank when you realised you were not right for the part. It was often the way that you had to conform to a casting director's idea of what a taxi-driver, vicar, or postman looked like, or, you had to match the family members who had already been cast. After forty years, I have given up trying to second-guess casting directors.

A few months later, I went for a casting for a programme called *Boy meets Girl*. I read for the part of the father of Rachel Stirling, who is the daughter of Diana Rigg. A few days later, they told me that I didn't get the part, as I looked too young. I was sixty-seven, and looked too young to be the father of a 30-year-old girl, what planet are these people on?

When my daughter Lucy was in *The Braithwaites*, they had to cast an actor to play her father. I was not in the running, as I was not well enough known and for the reason that, as she had red hair, they wanted to cast a red-headed man instead. That's all very well, but both Helen and I are dark haired. Nevertheless, the stereotypes are always used.

Even when you reached the dizzy heights of a 'recurring' character, there was still a downside. There was no way of knowing when you would be called upon. If you were unavailable when the call came, someone else would be booked and, in all probability, they would become the regular character from then on. Fifty 'vicars', just as competent as me are sitting watching every time I appear, and on one occasion a late booking caused problems. Lucy and Andrew had booked a long weekend in Prague for Helen and me as a present for my sixtieth birthday. The week before the holiday, Granada said they wanted me for a big storyline. The decision was mine, and in the event, we cancelled the holiday and lost all the money and I did the job for Granada. We did take the holiday a few weeks later, but there was friction, and it did cause me to think. Was there any way of knowing in advance if I was needed? It seemed not, I was at their beck and call and if I did not like it, there were plenty waiting impatiently behind me.

Some of the lengths people would go to at auditions were astounding. I was meeting a casting director called Michael Syers at a casting for a corporate video in Stockport. The casting was for a blind man again, and I thought that in view of my *Jimmy Grimble* experience, I had a chance. There were several of us waiting when a man came in with dark glasses and a white stick. I showed him to a seat and asked him if he would like me to read the script to him. He seemed grateful and I did my best to help him. When my turn came to be interviewed, I said to Michael, "it's not really fair you know, there's a real blind man waiting, he should get the job."

Michael looked at the man's name on the list and said: "I've known that fellow for twenty years, he's not blind at all." Funnily enough I got that job, so perhaps virtue is its own reward.

In my private life, things were fine, and I counted my blessings. Lucy was about to leave College and stated her intention to enter the world of theatre. Of course, we had tried to dissuade her, but remembering my own longings when I was younger, promised to help her all we could. Helen had tentatively tried to interest her in a teaching career, but she was adamant, and we gave in with as much grace as we could. She applied to several drama schools and prepared for the auditions.

This was the first time she had come up against the harsh realities of this business. The drama school auditions meant travelling maybe hundreds of miles, sometimes an overnight stay, to compete against possibly a couple of hundred other young hopefuls in a five-minute slot. Some of the applicants were returning for their second or even third year, so standards were fiercely high. It was hard not to think that the schools were treating these auditions as fund raising events, perhaps up to a couple of hundred teenagers paying £35 for the privilege of performing their pieces, and then to be told, "we'll let you know." To me, this borders on exploitation, and it leaves a bad taste.

Lucy was offered a place at Brunel University, to do a degree course in Theatre Studies and Drama and, whilst it wouldn't have been her first choice, she decided to take it and prepared to set off for London.

A part in *Emmerdale* came my way, so perhaps not saying anything to the casting director about mistaking Jimmy Grimble for Billy Elliot had been the right thing to do, although it still hurt. On the first day of my three-day shoot as a bogus doctor, I took some details of Lucy and handed them to the casting department. Of course, I was biased, but from what I had seen of Lucy's performances over the years in school, college, and local amateur shows, I thought she showed a lot of promise.

The following day the phone rang. It was Yorkshire TV asking Lucy to come to audition for a small part in *Emmerdale* as a Goth. She got the part and I thought that she acquitted herself well for her first appearance on television.

What we did not know at the time was that they wanted to try her out to see how she came across on screen. They were casting for a new family for a big upcoming series called *At Home with the Braithwaites*. They auditioned her four times for different parts. They were particularly interested in her flaming red hair and she was eventually offered the role of Tamsin, the lesbian girlfriend of one of the main characters, played by Sarah Smart.

When the series came out, Lucy became a little bit well known, something, which she never seemed comfortable with. Her ambition was to work in the theatre if possible. Off she went to University, and during the three years she spent at Brunel, she did the remaining three series of *The Braithwaites* to some acclaim.

By this time, I had been in the business for coming up to forty years, and due to my one bit of nepotism, had started my Lucy on the way to four series of a top rated drama. Ironically, I also played a part as a gardener in the same series, but with three lines, who said life was fair?

When my *Braithwaites* script arrived, the directions said that the gardener walked up with a wheelbarrow, stopped and delivered his lines. We were on holiday in France with some of our friends, Keith and David. They made me practise every day with a wheelbarrow which was around the 'Chateau' where we stayed, saying that they wanted a credit for 'gardener trainer'. On the morning of filming, I walked up with my wellies on, wheelbarrow in front. The director took one look and said, "lose the wheelbarrow, it looks ridiculous." I am not sure that David and Keith have ever recovered from the disappointment, but hey, that's show biz.

Lucy took her degree and set about finding work whilst living in London. Now the realities of this cruel business hit home, and although never complaining, she, like plenty of others took jobs in pubs and restaurants to survive. It is worse somehow for girls because they stand to be exploited by men. We used to go to London to see her and our hearts used to ache. After two years or so, she called us and asked if we would support her if she applied to take a PGCE, which, as she already had a degree in theatre and drama, would mean she would be a teacher after a one-year course.

Of course, we agreed, and Lucy applied to the prestigious Goldsmiths, and was accepted. After completing her year successfully, she worked for four years in a tough London comprehensive. For the first few months, she was in a bad way. My little girl, who stood five foot four, had to contend with sixteen-year-old streetwise kids who towered over her. There were times when she phoned Helen in tears, but eventually she gained the respect of her pupils, and coped superbly. Lucy does not complain. She just gets on with things and when I saw the conditions under which she worked, my admiration knew no bounds.

Some of Lucy's kids knew that she had appeared in *The Braithwaites*, and she asked if I would come and talk to them about acting. I took some videos and showed them, and they were fascinated that I had worked with Ray Winstone, who was a hero to them. When I asked for questions, they mainly wanted to know how much money I got, what was Ray like, and how did they get into acting? What struck me was that they all seemed to be over six feet and were 'well hard'. How Lucy coped five days a week was beyond me. I found it astonishing but gratifying, that they seemed to have a great deal of affection for her.

Lucy met her partner Joe when they were at Goldsmiths. He had been a journalist but had decided that teaching might give him more job satisfaction. Joe had been a Cambridge graduate and settled into teaching like a duck to water. He also taught in a tough south London comprehensive. After four years, they applied for a teaching post abroad. They were interviewed in London and both were offered jobs in a prestigious school in Kuala Lumpur. Off they went and were happily teaching there for five years. Helen and I went out for a month to see them in January. It was lovely to get away from the English winter. I could get used to it.

Lucy takes after Helen in her absolute honesty and integrity and, when I am feeling low, just thinking about her can make me smile and realise how lucky I am.

A Selection of Photographs
from the Author's Collection

With David Tennant on Casanova

Cookie and Thumbs, Home Fires

Jack Duckworth and Vicar, Vera's funeral

Bill Tarmey opens my shop

A pastoral visit to the Platts

Early Rogue Traders

The genius that is Jeremy Brett

Suranne Jones

My first speaking part with Rita

First day on Home Fires

With Meg on Sooty

On the set of Wild Bill

Panto with Roy Barraclough, Oldham Rep

An Emmerdale Wedding

25: Kiszko, Cracker, Cops

A labour of love is how someone described my next project, a television film about Stefan Kiszko. I met the director, Steven Whittaker, in Manchester and got the part of the Clerk of the Court for his trial. When I read the script, it was brought home to me what a terrifying miscarriage of justice could be caused by being the wrong person in the wrong place at the wrong time.

At the read through with the full cast in London, Steven Whittaker amazed everybody by knowing not just the names of all the characters in over one hundred and fifty scenes, but also every scene in which they appeared. He had done such a thorough job because he felt so incensed by the injustice of the case. An innocent man was locked up for 17 years and subjected to unimaginable humiliations and cruelties.

Steven had unearthed a fine young actor to play Kiszko. His name was Tony Maudsley. His performance moved us all to tears. The programme was called *A Life for a Life*. It starred the Hollywood Oscar winner Olympia Dukakis as Kiszco's mother. It was well received and quite deservedly, won awards for Tony.

Another audition, this time for *Cracker*, and I really wanted this one. I had been a fan of Robbie Coltrane since seeing him in a series called *Tutti Frutti*, which also featured Richard Wilson. It was set in the rather seedy world of rock and roll in Scotland, and was a very funny series.

In *Cracker*, Coltrane had made the part of the forensic psychologist his own, and had given Fitz many human failings, which endeared him to over twelve million viewers.

Hallelujah! I got the small role of the factory foreman in a particularly grisly episode. The guest 'star' of my episode was a young actor named John Simm. He did a fine job and was destined for many terrific roles.

Another young actor who was playing a policeman said, "hello, his name was Steve Huison, and he had two lines."

When I next saw him, he was surrounded by the cast of *City Central* in which he was playing a part. They were quizzing him about how he had been treated at the Oscars that year, and how people like Madonna had said how much they enjoyed his film. I had not seen it, but he had played a leading role in a film called *The Full Monty*, and as it had been Oscar nominated, the whole cast had been flown to LA and treated like kings. Steve is now a regular in *Coronation Street*, playing the feckless 'Eddie Windass'.

Interestingly at the read through, Robbie Coltrane made a special point of singling out the writer Paul Abbott for particular praise. This was not something that was routinely done, but in the years since then, I have realised what a fine and ground-breaking writer he is.

Next came a casting, which was a little different. It was for a new, gritty cop series, to be called *Cops*, and the auditions were to be in the form of improvisations. I quite liked improvising and fancied my chances. I was recalled four times over the next two weeks and each time the participants became fewer. On the final day, after what I thought was a good session for me, the director came over and put his arm around my shoulder. "How tall are you Jim?"

"Five nine" I answered.

"Great you'll just fit the uniform for the character." Crikey he had as good as told me I was in, and I went home on cloud nine.

I never heard from him again. I did not get the part, and I wonder to this day if I read too much into his comments.

The show was a great success, being shot almost in documentary fashion, and it proved a breakthrough for a man who I had been seeing at auditions for thirty years. John Henshaw is a lovely person and a fine character actor. For many a long year, John had been slogging around the audition 'circuit' with about the same degree of success as me, which was not a lot. Since *Cops*, he has gone from strength to strength; proof that perseverance and talent will out. I think his best work was in the wonderful *Early Doors*, where he played the pub landlord to perfection. Katy Cavanagh also had a breakthrough moment in the *Cops* series, and is now a regular in *Coronation Street*.

The co-operative agency was floundering. The main problem was that many of the actors did not want to do the office work and it was decided that we would disband. Perhaps it was just as well, because one thing I realised from working in the office was that co-ops seemed to be a last resort for casting people. Whenever we managed to get more than a cough or spit for someone, they left us and sought representation with commercial agencies, especially in London. None of us could blame them. We would all have done the same given the chance.

I was now without an agent, an unhappy situation.

26: A Doctor Appears

Perhaps the most rewarding and satisfying event of my life happened round about now. Andrew was sitting his final exams with some trepidation. It was good in a way that he was only forty miles away, because when he left home, I was lost. He had been my best mate. I consoled myself with the fact that he was fairly nearby, but as he found his feet at University, his visits home became less frequent. Because a medicine degree takes five years, he had been worried that a lot of the friends he had made at Sheffield were leaving after three years. In the event, he shared a house with three girl medics for his final two years. Helen and I were pleased about this because the girls turned out to be just the civilising influence he needed.

One day during his weekly phone call, he told us he had met a girl, and they were going out. The significance of this was not lost on us. He had never mentioned girlfriends before.

It had been a long haul for Andrew, and we had everything crossed in the hope that he would be OK. Things had not come easily to Andrew either. He was undoubtedly bright, but he would be the first to admit, he was not a genius. He was also a laid back individual. Nothing bothers him for long and if he has a setback, he just gets up and tries again. On the day he phoned from Sheffield and told me that he was now a doctor, I put the phone down and had a little cry. I could not help but think of Sara my mum, and the times she sat all night sewing buttons. She was long dead, but how proud she would have been.

Helen was at school with special dispensation to keep her mobile phone on. She was as happy as I was, and once again I realised that in the important things, I was so fortunate.

Something that occurred to me was that Andrew was now twenty-three. When I was twenty-three, I had been working, for eight years! Another thing was, I was the only one in our house without a degree. A taxi driver in a family full of eggheads, unbearable.

One thing Helen and I had done which was to prove to be a lifesaver financially was to buy a big house. When things were going well at the shop, we saw a detached house go up for sale in the same drive as we lived. We had a chat about it, and decided to go for broke. Getting a mortgage was not such a problem then, as I was classed as a businessman, and not an actor. Because we had a big mortgage, we never seemed to have much money, but struggled through. We loved the house, as did the kids. It had an enormous garden, and Lucy used to wander down to her 'singing' tree, or her 'reading' tree. Once the two of them had left home, it was miles too big for just two of us, so we put it on the market.

It took eighteen months to sell. We bought a semi almost next to our original house. So, we had moved to three houses in the same drive, must be the wanderlust in us. At last we had no mortgage, and the pressure was finally easing.

27: Royal Exchange, Reverend Todd

I looked through the list of actors' agents in Manchester. It was always difficult to get an agent to take you on unless you were well known, but I felt that as I had by now amassed nearly forty years in the business, admittedly without any long term success, I had something to offer. I had to be careful. This would probably be my last chance.

Talking to other actors, the name of Elizabeth Stocking at the Narrow Road Agency kept coming up. She was reckoned to be a caring and efficient person who used to work at Granada TV, and I applied to her agency. She was always busy when I rang, and I took a chance one morning and just said that I was coming into Manchester on some errand and would call on her. This is not something I would normally do, but luckily for me Elizabeth interviewed me, and we got on very well.

She took me on, and has been my agent ever since. Agents are not miracle workers and if there are no enquiries coming in, there is only so much they can do, but the knowledge that someone really is looking out for you is what matters, and I count myself fortunate.

The first call from Elizabeth was to attend the Royal Exchange Theatre in Manchester to read for the small part of Tubby Wadlow in *Hobson's Choice*. I said, "I don't think they like me at The Exchange. I've been there four times for auditions without getting the job."

She replied, "if they didn't like you darling, they would have only seen you once. Get down there and do your best."

The Royal Exchange is a sort of Holy Grail for northern-based actors such as me, and I trotted off there to see the great man himself, Braham Murray. I was very well prepared for this interview. *Hobson's Choice* was set in Salford and chronicled some of the privations of working-class people who played the employees in the shop. I had studied the script and empathised with them. Although set a century earlier, the memories of my childhood and the sense of deprivation said something to me, and I took along my own interpretation of the role.

Braham seemed interested and, instead of seeing him for the usual ten minutes, I was auditioned for over half an hour. He made me read the part three or four times, and discussed the feelings of me – a Salford lad – and what I could bring to the role. When I had finished, he thanked me for coming and told me to take the script with me as I left.

I knew that I had made an impression and was as confident as I had ever been about an audition, so the disappointment was more painful than usual when I did not get it. The message that came back was that the character of Tubby had to be played by someone who could 'double', and understudy Trevor Peacock, who was playing Hobson, and it went to a fine actor Colin Prockter, who was much more experienced than me. When I saw the production, with John Thomson as Willie Mossop, I thought it was terrific. I would have loved to have been in it.

Helen and I are very fond of the Royal Exchange and try to see everything there. This is helped by a scheme, which, as far as we know, is unique, and round the stage are a series of 'banquettes.' Tickets for these are not allowed to be sold until the morning of each performance. We think that these are the best seats in the house and for the princely sum of eight quid, we have been within touching distance of Albert Finney, Tom Courtney, Trevor Peacock, and many more.

Without doubt, one of the best performances of recent years at the Exchange was that of Pete Postlethwaite as Prospero in *The Tempest*. We saw it on the press night, which is when all the people who are famous, or like to be seen around at openings, turn up. Having paid our usual eight quid, we were sitting amongst tons of sand, almost on stage. I was mesmerised by Postlethwaite's performance, I love his style of understated acting, and he was enthralling.

The following day, I was listening to the Simon Mayo show on *Radio Five Live*, and Pete came on to be interviewed, and talk about the play. I phoned just to pass a comment on the show. Ten minutes later my phone rang, and a voice asked if I would like to talk to Pete live on air. I agreed, and had a ten-minute chat during which I said that I was an admirer of 'unshowy' acting, and that I had sat with tears in my eyes and sand between my toes. He was charming and I enjoyed the bit of excitement.

Twice since I have been seen for auditions at the Exchange, without success, and I think that now my time for any employment there may have passed.

On a light-hearted note, my next role was in *Sooty*. I had remembered Sooty from the early days of TV, when that nice 'Mr Corbett' had his hand in the proceedings. I was to play an old tramp, begging under the local viaduct. Two days before the filming day, someone rang to ask if I could find a dog to bring with me. Our friends Jean and Tony had always kept dogs, and their current one was a delightful, good-natured little border collie. Tony took a day off work and accompanied me to the location and Meg acquitted herself like a little star. The nice thing for Jean and Tony is that they now have a permanent record on film of the now departed Meg.

My next call was yet again to be auditioned at Granada. Once again for a vicar. Once again in *Coronation Street*. The interview was with John Anderson, and I realised when I read the bit of script that contained my part, that this was a giant storyline. My meeting with John went very well, and a week later they rang to offer me the part.

Of course, I was over the moon and when the script arrived it was accompanied by a very strong letter, which told me under no circumstances, was I to discuss the plot with anyone. This told me that it was a big storyline and I became even more excited. The story was the proposed wedding of Steve McDonald and his fiancée Karen. The wedding would be disrupted by Tracy Barlow, who ran into the church and denounced Steve as the father of her child, and the wedding was halted.

I had fourteen scenes, more than I had ever done on Corrie, and one in particular stood out. Steve and Karen had taken on board the fact that Steve had been unfaithful and was the father of Tracy's child. They had decided to continue with the marriage ceremony because they loved each other. The vicar thought otherwise, and had to remind them that marriage was not something to be taken lightly. The whole scene was taken up with the stating of the various viewpoints and the vicar was eventually persuaded to marry them. At last, some real 'acting' for me in *Coronation Street*. I studied my script intently, and learned the whole wedding ceremony by heart.

The first day of any shoot is always a nervous time. Once again, doubts encompassed me. I did not sleep very well and turned up for my costume, wardrobe and make-up check at 6.00am. I was sure that my big scene would be towards the end of the five days at the lovely Arley Hall near Warrington. The rest of the cast and crew were already there, having started filming the day before. A chauffeur-driven Mercedes was waiting for me, and we set off in the rush hour traffic. As we sped up the motorway, the driver's phone rang. I heard one half of a conversation, which was obviously about me.

"Yes, I've got him in the back," the driver said. "Well I'm going as fast as I can, but the traffic is pretty bad. OK, I'll be there as soon as possible." He put down his phone and said, "They're waiting for you."

Now the nerves really kicked in. We screeched into Arley Hall and were met by Peter Shaw, a senior assistant director at Granada who I had known for many years. "Hello Jim," he said. "Lovely to see you again, sorry to rush you, but we are ready for Steve and Karen's scene where they want the marriage to go ahead." Oh no, I thought, they were shooting out of sequence and this difficult scene was first up.

We went into the church to be greeted by a sort of organised chaos. There were two film cameras to shoot the Corrie bit from different angles, a film crew from *GMTV*, and a film crew from *This Morning*. Thirty members of the main cast, twenty extras, various technicians, make-up, wardrobe, and sound departments were milling about, all waiting for me.

John Anderson greeted us and said we would rehearse the lines. I was hyperventilating and hoped that no one noticed. I fluffed the first line run. The second was not much better, and panic started to set in. On the third run, Simon Gregson, who plays Steve made an unholy mess of his lines. Ha, I thought, even he can't get his lines, which made me feel a bit better. Fourth run and Suranne Jones, who played Karen, stumbled badly over her speech. "Gawd, I'm always doing that. I don't know how I keep my job," she said, and we all had a bit of a laugh. I was relaxing somewhat now, and after a few adjustments for lighting and sound, we shot the scene.

I didn't realise until after we had broken for lunch and the scene was in the can, that Suranne and Simon had messed up their lines on purpose. They had realised that I was in a terrible state and did it to settle me down. I tried to thank Simon over the next few days, but when I mentioned it to him, he just smiled. Once again, what some might see as a small kindness had left me with something I would never forget.

The rest of the shoot was a joy. I relaxed into my role and the week sped by. One thing that always amused me was the fact that whenever I joined the line for food at the catering van, the techies who might have been using 'industrial' language always stopped swearing. I laughingly tried to explain that I wasn't really a man of the cloth, but it must have been the 'dog collar ' because it happened every time.

I shared a Winnebago with Andrew Whyment, who played Kirk, and found him great company. The fact that he was a Man United fan, gave us plenty to talk about.

Whilst waiting for a camera set up, I had a long chat with Barbara Knox, and we reminisced about the music hall so many years before.

Anne Kirkbride was as entertaining as ever and kept us laughing. I didn't have the nerve to remind her of her 'schoolgirl antics' in our music hall. It brought home to me how much time had passed. The Oldham Rep show had been 1973 and we were now in 2003.

One night after a long day in front of the cameras, I shared a car home with Bill Roache. In real life, Bill has always seemed to be quite a reserved character and, although he was always scrupulously polite and friendly, he intimidated me somewhat. If he seemed tired, or remote, I wouldn't bother him with chatter, but he appeared to be quite happy to talk.

I chatted to him about my first appearance, my few lines so long ago, and how the tension used to rise as the twelve-minute segment, which used to comprise a half of one programme, ticked by. He told me that when he first started, *Coronation Street* was transmitted live. LIVE, to twenty million viewers, now that's pressure. The drive back to the studios was about an hour and we were both soon asleep. The chauffeur told us that we had caused a couple of quizzical glances when he stopped at lights: Ken Barlow and a vicar fast asleep in the back of a car.

My happy week came to an end, and I was really pleased with my work. I realised once again that my main dialogue would not be seen, as naturally whilst the boring old vicar was waffling on, important plot revelations were taking place. Nonetheless, he played an important part in the overall scheme of things, and John Anderson seemed quite pleased.

When the episode was transmitted, it had viewing figures of seventeen million. The biggest non-sport TV figures of the year.

I was now a little more used to the inevitable bit of depression that followed such an exciting week, but I was also glad of a rest. How people did this full time was beyond me.

A couple of months later, I landed a lovely juicy role in the police series set in Manchester, called *City Central*. This is where I met Steve Huison again. I was playing a deranged man who murdered a loan shark with a cricket bat. One of the regular policewomen in the series was a little Scottish girl, and my scenes with her made me realise that she was a really fine actress. She was called Ashley Jensen, and it is no surprise she has gone on to greater things. A couple of years later, I failed to get a part in *Extras*. That was disappointing as it would have been great to work with her again. Also, the programme *Extras* portrayed with painful clarity, the reality of the background artist. I used to squirm as I watched it, remembering my own experiences.

Another role I did not get was that of an Irish Priest in *Max and Paddy's Adventures*, but I did get to meet Peter Kay who was casting it. I was a great admirer, especially of *Phoenix Nights*. The well-observed club scenes made me laugh out loud. Any club 'turn' would have recognised Kay as Brian Potter, the owner of the Phoenix. He could be a concert secretary from a hundred clubs in which I appeared. They were essentially working lads given a bit of power over the acts, and some of them did not let you forget it.

28: Deaf Barry

My agent Elizabeth phoned one morning. "Got an audition for you luvvie, with the BBC." *Goodie*, I thought. "London I'm afraid," she said. "Some kind of northern drama, get there early and have a read of the script."

My interview was for 12.20 at BBC White City, so if I got the 8.25am train from Manchester, I would get to Euston with plenty of time to get the tube. The crowd waiting at platform six told me that something was wrong and when I found a man in a red Virgin Trains' waistcoat I asked where the 8.25 train was.

"Stuck at Longsight for repairs, Sir."

"But I've got to get to London, it's important."

"I know what you're going to say Sir, and I agree with you completely, but the 8.25 is cancelled and there's nothing I can do."

I left a panicky message on my agent's answerphone and caught a train through Wolverhampton and Birmingham, which got me to Euston at 12.20pm, arriving at the BBC forty minutes late for my interview.

I met the director, Julie Ann Robinson, and the casting lady. They were very sympathetic about trains and my – by now – dishevelled appearance, and I read for the part, all four lines of it. We discussed what sort of character 'Deaf Barry' might be, and ten minutes later I was heading for the tube and Euston.

For the hundredth time, I wondered about the economics of this job, taking a day off from taxi driving, train and tube tickets costing me a total of £120 on the day. Forty years I've been at it, and it doesn't get any easier.

When you are wanted for a part you normally hear within a couple of days. I didn't hear anything and had given up on this job. Then Elizabeth called and told me they wanted me to be 'Deaf Barry' and would send me the scripts over. Ten weeks work over the next six months was not to be sneezed at, even if it was a local programme.

That evening, I answered the phone at home. A voice said, "Jim Whelan, this is Jim Cole, from the BBC, first assistant director on *Blackpool*. Please put my number in your phone. You must ring me anytime, day or night, over the next six months if you have any problems."

I thought that this was a bit over the top and asked who else was in the programme: David Morrissey, Sarah Parrish, David Tennant, John Thomson, Steve Pemberton, Georgia Taylor – WOW! This was not a local programme with names like that. Perhaps I had struck lucky.

The read-through is always one of the best days. It's the only time when everyone involved with the production, is in the same place at the same time. About eighty people met in a church hall in Hammersmith: actors, director, camera and sound people, wardrobe, make-up, accountant and casting, and we read through episodes one to three. Because my part was relatively small, I read in for two others who were unable to be there. One of the actors was at the 'National ', and the other was filming elsewhere.

During a coffee break, a man I didn't know tapped me on the shoulder. "Hi Jim, how do you see Deaf Barry's character evolving?" Trying to think on my feet, I mumbled something about a stupid haircut and unhappy childhood for Barry, and gently enquired who he was.

"Pete Bowker, the writer."

Oh God, had I said the wrong thing? Having met me, would he think I am not right for the part and have me removed? I spent the next half hour brown nosing in a desperately ingratiating fashion. Why do I do that? Aren't I a prat? I wonder if he even noticed.

We were also introduced to a choreographer and told that there would be dance rehearsals for the next three days. I didn't know we were going to dance.

On the first day of shooting, I was picked up from my hotel and taken to a location in Bushey, where, after getting into costume and having my head sheared by make-up, I met the other four actors in the scene. It seemed surreal. I was working with David Morrissey, John Thomson, Sarah Parrish and David Tennant – four famous actors and me. I was petrified. Anytime anyone called my name for make-up or wardrobe, I thought *Oh no, I've been found out, they're gonna sack me.* Does every actor feel this desperate insecurity and unworthiness, I wonder?

We got a few takes in the can and I could relax a bit. It became clear that David Morrissey is a bit special. He exuded a kind of energy and menace as Ripley Holden, and as my 'Deaf Barry' was the man who worked for Holden, it seemed clear that I would be awfully close to him over the next six months. What a result.

After two weeks shooting exteriors in London and then Blackpool, we went to a custom-built set of Ripley's arcade on an industrial estate in Perivale. The set itself was stupendous: hundreds of arcade machines of all kinds, and enough bulbs to light a small town. We were to spend five weeks there. Twelve-hour days, six days a week.

Upstairs were dressing rooms and a shabby 'green room' area with a grotty looking pool table. The studio was not air-conditioned and, as the weather outside warmed up, the temperature in the studio soon rose above 100°F. Five portable air-conditioners arrived but did not seem to make much difference. Most of the cast were in costumes for the Blackpool exteriors for continuity reasons. I didn't have many big scenes so I was all right and could sit outside half of the day. The principals just seemed to get on with it and nothing fazed Morrissey who just produced the goods, take after take.

The dancers arrived for one of the big production numbers. They could listen to the instructions from the choreographer Michelle, and remember steps immediately, but to us actors it was a case of repetition. Still we consoled ourselves that our 'characters' wouldn't be 'proper' dancers. With a dozen dancers, fifteen actors, thirty extras, about fifty crew and with the glow from the machines and film lighting, the heat was unbearable. The make-up girls were continually mopping our brows. Two days of this was enough, and we were relieved when the numbers were done.

David Tennant arrived. He played Ripley Holden's adversary, Policeman DC Carlisle. What an actor! I watched their scenes. They batted their lines back and forth like shuttlecocks; the slightest change of inflection here and there, creating tension and excitement. They reminded me of two boxers, evenly matched, both at the top of their game. I watched with wonder. My sense of inadequacy, never far from the surface, assailed me.

The production seemed to have taken on a life of its own. Everybody, maybe one hundred people were pulling in the same direction. It was clear that we all thought, rightly or wrongly, that something exciting was happening. In my dark moments, I wondered if the British public would accept musical numbers and dancing as an integral part of the action, but my doubts were forgotten when I saw some of the performances.

Our director was Julie Anne Robinson. She had been involved since the beginning of the project and interviewed me and gave me the job. She worked a fourteen-hour day, having to be in the studio at the start to plan shots, direct everything during the day, and she was the last to leave at the close of the shoot. I did not have an awful lot of contact – being mostly in the background, but could turn to her for advice when my close-ups arrived. She looked knackered – no wonder.

One day, I had lines and for a brief period, I was the centre of everyone's world. We had a couple of rehearsals of dialogue and left them to light the scene. I had learned these lines backwards, forwards, and sideways, so that I didn't slip up and spoil a shot. There were two film cameras pointing at me, soundmen sticking booms at me, make-up powdering my nose, props and continuity at me, as well as a script person checking what I said. I took deep breaths, told myself I must not panic, and hoped that no one would notice my trembling. "Action!" The take wasn't quite right, there was a shadow somewhere. "Action!" I made a slight fluff, drunk some water. "Action! Jim, you moved your head in the wrong direction." Both cameramen gave me orders at the same time I got confused. Panic was not far away.

"Just a minute, you're both talking to him at once." David Morrissey stuck up for me. He'd got the status to say that, I hadn't, or maybe I just didn't have the bottle.

"Action!" That was better we were getting there. "Action! Super that's the one."

I'm so relieved, that I nearly kiss Morrissey. What is it that makes us do this? Why am I drawn to this terrifying ordeal? My courage started to return, and my other shots went OK, but when I got back to the hotel and tried to watch the England match on TV, I was comatose in minutes.

We were by halfway through by now. Julie Anne finished her three episodes and while she edited these, we had a new director. I felt lost because Julie Anne gave me the job and I was going to miss her. I could not really put into words how grateful I was, and so clumsily gave her a hug and said goodbye.

Our new director was Coky Giedroyc. She was a slim, lovely looking girl and I wondered if she would be able to handle such a big production. My fears were soon laid to rest when an altercation occurred on her first day, and she put the person firmly in his place. She was the boss.

We finished the arcade shoot and went to Blackpool for a couple of weeks and then back to London. We were nearing the end now, and I arrived at the Rivoli ballroom in Lewisham for a massive wedding scene, which was the climax of the show. As well as our 'regular' dancers we were augmented by ballroom dancers. I'm always struck by the fact that all these extras have their own agenda. One young girl was a second-year medical student using her dancing skills to earn a bit of money.

This scene was massive and included all sorts of dance and musical numbers as well as resolving conflicts between the main characters. Michelle, the choreographer, had her work cut out trying to bring the actors up to scratch so that we did not stick out like sore thumbs. Director Coky had to try to organise dramatic scenes during, in between, and around the numbers. We now had three cameras and loads of extra people and it was like Fred Karno's in there, but somehow the adrenalin started to flow and, bit-by-bit, things started to take shape. I suppose the secret was that everyone knew their jobs and when someone called "Action!" we all worked to the same end, but sometimes it just seemed like a miracle that two hundred people could combine to make thirty seconds of film.

Georgia Taylor from Corrie was the bride. She looked both beautiful and vulnerable in her wedding dress.

On our last day in the ballroom, something happened that will stay with me. Ripley had to make a long speech from the stage about how he's messed up his life. David Morrissey performed to two hundred people, half of whom had not a clue who his character was, and yet many of them were in tears. Six times he repeated it for technical reasons, and every time he moved them. How does he do that? What is the secret? I can only admire from afar.

We were saying goodbye to loads of people, but I had another week to go, and it was so sad. Actors were called out on to the dance floor individually, and everybody clapped and cheered. I tried not to think of my last day.

My final morning, and the number one driver, Terry, in the number one car, the Lexus, normally allocated to David, picked me up. It was a nice gesture, but it would take more than that to make me emotional. During the lunch break, I said goodbye to people in the crew and my little make-up girl, Cat, wiped her eyes. Chatting to David Morrissey in between scenes, he admitted that he was worn out and would be glad of a rest.

I sat on my own whilst they lit the last scene. When the director Coky, put an arm around me and said, "Aw Jim, you're leaving today; we'll miss you," I was in floods of tears. She patted me on the shoulder and left me alone, and people turned away. All my good intentions were gone. I felt such a fool. I wish I hadn't done that.

Now that it was all done and dusted, questions remained. Was our programme any good? Have we been kidding ourselves? Would the music and dancing work? We would find out soon.

After it had finished, I was desolate. I couldn't let it go. It now all seemed like a dream. During the shoot, I used to experience surges of pure happiness for no reason. Perhaps drama is my fix; maybe I cannot let go because I'm addicted to the excitement, the buzz, and the terror – who knows?

When transmitted, *Blackpool* received generally good notices. Some critics thought that it was one of the best programmes of the year, and it was nominated for a Bafta.

I thought this might be my only chance to go to the Baftas, and I left messages on various answerphones at the BBC, of people who had been so friendly. Not receiving a single return call, I decided to phone the Bafta offices. A nice lady told me how much she had enjoyed the programme, and said that she could reserve me two tickets for the theatre for £450 each. I made my excuses and hung up. Once again, I was put firmly in my place.

One instance of 'star power', tickled me during the filming. We had been rehearsing some dancing numbers in a studio in Chelsea, and we finished at 5.30pm. Georgia Taylor said she wanted to go back home to Manchester, and we got the tube together to Euston. The 6.45 train is always packed to the roof, because it is the first train that people can get with 'day return', or cheap tickets. Georgia could easily have travelled first class and charged the BBC, but she said that she never liked to take advantage. We could not get seats and finished up sitting on the filthy floor. As people passed, they recognised Georgia as Toyah from Corrie, and some unkind remarks were uttered. After ten minutes of this, I went forward into the first-class compartment, to be met by a Virgin train manager who asked me where I was going. I said to him, "do you remember Toyah from *Coronation Street*?"

He said: "Yes, of course."

I said: "Well she's sitting on the filthy floor back there and I think it's disgraceful."

His manner changed in a heartbeat, and he went and brought her up to first class. Georgia was embarrassed but grateful. She would never trade on her name like that, but I did. We were treated to free coffee all the way home. The only drawback was that we had to suffer the train manager telling us his life story for two and a half hours.

While I was still fresh from *Blackpool*, it was a good time to be auditioned and I had high hopes when Elizabeth sent me the script for a new comedy written by Dave Spikey. I thought that it was sensational and very funny. It was called *Dead Man Weds*, and the part I was up for was the old duffer editor of the local newspaper in whose offices it was set. Meeting Dave Spikey was lovely. He was another of my local heroes, and had worked for years as a haematologist at Bolton Royal Hospital before co writing *Phoenix Nights* with Peter Kay. He is also one of the funniest stand-ups in the country, and is constantly touring to sell out audiences.

I thought that I interviewed quite well, and had to go to London for the next stage, a re-call. Once again, I felt OK, but heard a week later that 'my' part had gone to Alan Rothwell, a former original from *Coronation Street*, and much better known than me.

In the event, the series was a major disappointment, seeming to lose a lot of its humour and charm somewhere in the process of filming. The script, which I had thought so funny, came out clunky and lifeless, and I wondered how that could happen? It is hard to locate what goes wrong with a project, why would a wonderful script turn into a leaden set of performances? Where would the rot set in, would the actors know that they were in a stinker? Is it the director?

I don't know the answers, and I think that not many others do either – witness *Heartbeat* – a series which was apparently 'dead in the water', became a much loved Sunday night dose of 'cocoa television,' and remained an ITV staple for many years.

29: Taxi Driving

I went back to my taxi.

Driving people around all day gives you an insight in to how people tick. Most folks just want to get from A to B as quickly and cheaply as possible. Some treat you like dirt, and some are very considerate. When *Blackpool* was transmitted, I received some publicity and, on the rare occasions people recognised me, usually because they already knew my face from being regulars in my taxi, they were perplexed. "How come you are driving people about if you are on telly"?

It was hard to try and tell people that a film or telly part every couple of months would not pay the bills. They think the fact that you were in a film meant you were rich

Taxi drivers are a unique breed. The fact that the income is not guaranteed, and that you can go for hours, sitting around and not making a penny, makes us a bit paranoid. When a job comes through, we are in such a rush to get it done, that the tendency to speed is always there. Helen always said that I was a more dangerous driver when I was taxiing.

Driving a taxi, of course, meant being self-employed. I tried – not always successfully – to record all my takings; the temptation was always present to under-declare. I had an accountant who made sure I never got myself in trouble, but I have lost count of the number of drivers who found themselves the subject of tax investigations. Whilst never condoning any avoidance, my sympathies were firmly with the drivers. Many had to work up to sixteen hours a day to make it pay and nearly always, if the choice was between declaring and feeding their family, the tax was not paid. I knew very few drivers who retired with either a nest egg, or a decent pension.

It also keeps your feet on the ground. My local paper the *Bury Times*, had done an article on my involvement over the years as a vicar in *Coronation Street*, and the other drivers were giving me plenty of 'stick 'about it. One morning I was despatched to pick up a regular passenger from our local Marks and Spencer. I pulled up beside her and noticed a 'hoodie 'and his girlfriend near to the car. He mumbled something as he passed, and I thought I had better take no notice. The lady got into the car and asked me if I had heard what he had said? When I said not, she said that he had snarled, "There's that twat off the telly."

Fame at last!

Christmas of that year, and we were looking forward to Andrew and Lucy both being home with us in Bury. A tired sounding Andrew phoned a couple of weeks before and told us that he was unable to get the time off. He was just coming to the end of a six month stint in A&E, and his superior had informed him that, in spite of the fact he had booked this week's leave five months ago, if he went home there would be no cover and only one poor junior doctor to work over Christmas. This kind of emotional blackmail was seemingly the 'norm' in the National Health Service and, the fact that government edicts were always appearing stating that junior doctors' hours were supposed to be reduced, never seemed to be what happened in practice.

We decided that the best thing to do was to go to Brighton and so we all spent Christmas in Andrew and Ruth's small flat. He cooked Christmas dinner, and seemed to me for the first time ever to be quite cynical about things. I realised later that this was his reaction to six months on A&E duty, and when he told us some of the stories, it is not really surprising.

On one weekend night, Andrew was stitching a deep gash in a drunken man's face. He asked what had happened, and the fellow said, "I was knocking seven kinds of shit out of him when he got me in the face with his belt buckle."

Andrew was then called to treat a person with similar injuries in the next cubicle, and this time the man said, "He was killing me until I got my belt off and smashed him in the face with the buckle." They were in adjoining beds.

We spent Christmas day together and then he went to work on Boxing Day, but at least he had New Year's Eve to look forward to as he was finishing at 10.00pm. When we spoke to him in the New Year, he said that as things had 'kicked off' in Brighton he worked until 6.00am.

When his A&E duty finished in February, he was soon back to his cheerful optimistic self. My admiration and love for him knows no bounds. I still pinch myself when I realise what he has achieved.

30: Casanova & Cambridge

I was dropping some passengers at Manchester airport when my agent's assistant Tiffany, called in some agitation to ask me where I was. When I told her, she asked me how long it would take me to get down to Granada studios. I said I could make it in half an hour. "Get straight down there and go to the *Casanova* set, someone's been taken ill, and they need a replacement immediately."

Of course, this was good for me, but not for the poor actor who had gone to hospital. I arrived and was greeted by David Tennant, who I had admired so much in *Blackpool*. "You've got ten minutes to learn your script Jim, they want to take down these sets tonight and we have to get this in the can."

There were half a dozen lines, lots of different positions for the character, and in some ways, it was the usual actor's nightmare of being turfed on to the stage naked.

It wasn't my finest hour. My nerves were shot, and the director was not at all sympathetic. David was kindness itself, and kept reminding me that it would cost tens of thousands if they had to wait another day. Each of my scenes took seven or eight takes, my ultimate dread, the technicians were looking away, the make-up girls couldn't keep the sweat from my brow and when we finished, I felt thoroughly miserable.

The character was needed for another day's work a week later. This time, I had the script in time and had learned it. Still, I was apprehensive about going. When I arrived everyone was sweetness and light, and even the director Sherry Folkson greeted me warmly. I realised that on the previous occasion everyone was under the most intense pressure and perhaps I should not have been so sensitive.

A month later, I had a call from the production office of *Casanova*, asking my permission to 'dub' my voice. Apparently, I wasn't sounding posh enough for them. Of course I agreed. When one of my badminton cronies who was my biggest critic saw my performance, he said "well that's the best bit of acting you've ever done, it didn't even sound like you." I didn't enlighten him.

The series was a great personal triumph for David Tennant; he of course went on to be the new *Doctor Who* but his was no overnight success. We had seen him some years previously as a prince in *Richard the Third* at the Royal Exchange and even then, it was obvious that he was a fine actor.

I love to tell people that I 'discovered' David, and gave him that all-important little 'push' after *Blackpool*. The truth is, I played one game of pool against him in our grotty green room. There was never doubt that given any sort of decent break, he would conquer the business.

Andrew called from Brighton where he was working at the Royal Sussex Hospital. He had been with Ruth since they met whilst he was studying at Sheffield. When Andrew qualified, Ruth was at London University. She was studying to be an Occupational Therapist, and Andrew wanted to be near her. The Brighton job came up, he took it and when Ruth qualified, they moved in together.

Helen and I loved Ruth dearly, and the call was to tell us that they had decided to marry. We were absolutely delighted.

Ruth was originally from Cambridge and her mum still lived in the area. They had found out that it was possible to have the reception in a College, and had been to check it out. They decided on Gonville and Caius College and Helen and I went to see it.

To walk through the gate into the quad was a salutary experience for me.

As far as I was concerned it was like entering another world. We wandered around the beautiful grounds, and I looked in amazement at the manicured lawns and portraits of famous people who were graduates. The one thing that impressed me most was Stephen Hawking's legacy.

Andrew and Ruth married in Cambridge and the reception took place in the Great Hall.

One thing that struck me straight away at the reception was the price of drinks. There was a picture of a glass of wine behind the bar, and the price said £4. One of my Irish relatives said that he thought this was a bit steep. The barman informed him that was the price of a bottle. We were paying student prices and you have never seen so many Irishmen wandering around Cambridge blissfully inebriated. Medics are also known for their fondness of the amber nectar, and the bar staff told us it had been a record night.

My heart swelled with pride and once again I wondered what Sara, my mum, would have thought. Maybe she does know?

Just over a year later, we found out Ruth was pregnant. Whilst I was as happy as anything for them, I knew that nothing could ever come close to the love I had for Andrew and Lucy. All these feelings went out of the nearest window when Ruth just came and plonked my grandson Ben in my arms. The joy Helen and I have in our Grandboys has been and remains so potent and intense. Ben seemed to like me, and as he grew, we became so close. I just adore him, and it was such a wrench when they moved to New Zealand, He has just become a teenager, a fine and good-looking lad.

31: Jason & Sarah

My next call came to play the Corrie vicar again. This time it was to pay a pastoral call to the Platt household and to try and set a date for the wedding of Jason and Sarah. It was nice to play a more intimate scene, especially as my interaction this time was with Gail, Jason, Sarah, and especially 'bad boy', David Platt.

The director was Duncan Foster, who I knew from *Emmerdale*. He made me feel at home and the couple of small scenes seemed to go well. A bonus for me was to act with Helen Worth, who plays Gail, She is a fine and underrated actress who knows what she wants and is extremely professional. The fact that I, as the vicar, was involved in setting a possible wedding date meant that I might hope for more work later that year. The significance of getting the part without having to audition was a great breakthrough for me. It meant that after a mere forty or so years of appearing in Corrie, I seemed to be a small, but 'recurring' character.

The next bit of excitement was to play a nice part in *The Royal*, without audition. I could not figure out why, until I received the script and found that the director was Duncan Foster. It is nice to be remembered for being a reliable actor by a director and to be given the part.

We filmed in Bradford, where a disused part of St Luke's Hospital had been fitted out as a 1960s' ward. A bonus for me was to meet up again with Michael Starke, with whom we had had such fun in *Brookside* some years before. The 1960s' set was a fascinating museum piece, and was truly authentic. How much things had changed, was brought home to us by a small incident. There was a dial telephone on the set. A ten-year-old girl who was vising the set and was the daughter of one of the regular actors, wandered up to it. She moved the dial around and asked us what it was. We explained as best we could, but she just looked more confused. She could not get how it worked and walked off shaking her head.

In this programme, I played a farmer who had been trodden on by a bull, and played a scene with Wendy Craig, what a pleasure. When the programme transmitted, one of my badminton cronies was heard to say that the best performance in the show was from the injured foot! Everyone is a critic.

Panto time again, and would I like to play dame? Yes, I certainly would, and I set about assimilating my costumes. In the small shows, which I played, artistes often had to provide their own garb, and my first call was to my mate David Williams. He had played dame in something like thirty shows over the years and he lent me some dresses, some boots, and very importantly, padded bra and comedy knickers. I had to keep my eyes open for size nine court shoes and caught sight of a pair in a charity shop. I went in and asked if I could try them on. The woman was very shirty, thinking that I was a cross dresser and was not convinced when I tried to tell her that I was playing the part of dame in panto.

The costumes were a bargain at four quid, and I took them home and sprayed them silver. Over the years, they have given me sterling service.

After the show was over, I was talking to David on the phone and I said that I would come to his house the following day and return his bra and knickers. I hope no one was listening to the call.

The call from Coronation Street came later that year for the Jason and Sarah wedding. Once again, when the scripts arrived, the strong letter not to discuss the plot accompanied them.

The excitement in this storyline was whether the wedding would even continue after David had done his best to disrupt proceedings by crashing his car into the canal. It was lovely this time to see that Michael Starke was now in Corrie as the father of a new family. He seemed to suit the role, and appeared set for a long run, but as happens so many times if the family does not gel, the powers that be can be ruthless, and Mike eventually left.

We were filming at the usual St Mary's church in Prestwich. When we arrived, there were twenty or so Paparazzi scattered about. Some of them had even climbed up the trees surrounding the churchyard.

Our caravans were about fifty yards from the church, but even so, we had cars to transport us to the location to frustrate the 'paps'. Anne Kirkbride asked me if I would walk with her to the church so that she could have a fag. As we walked out on to the street, arms linked to walk the fifty yards, the photographers pounced. This was the first time I had been 'papped', and it was a bit unnerving. Anne just laughed and said I would be 'exposed' as her mystery man in the tabloids.

For the following four days every scene featured the vicar, and once again I was treated like a regular member of the cast.

The director was again, Duncan Foster. Early in the shoot, he asked if it might be possible to run the whole of the wedding in one take. This was highly unusual, and it would only be used as a 'master' shot to cut to, during the episode. I had received the script some two weeks before, and thought that I could manage it, but to shoot a six-and-a-half-minute scene was almost unheard of. The dialogue was all from the vicar as Jason and Sarah would be only repeating what he said as responses. Of course, my nerves returned, but as I was wandering around the altar mumbling my lines to myself while they lit the set, a giant shout came from among the congregation, "stop mumbling to yourself Jim, you know it." This elicited a huge laugh and, of course. It was none other than Anne Kirkbride. The tension had gone, and so with some trepidation, Duncan said "action" and we started.

As the 'ceremony' continued, I grew in confidence and as we progressed, it was as if they really were getting married. With thirty or so regulars, and twenty extras, we had a 'real' congregation. When I finally pronounced them man and wife, everyone broke into a spontaneous round of applause. Although we had filmed a 'happy' conclusion to the day, it was by no means certain what would happen in the storyline, and the papers were in a froth trying to find out.

Helen had a former pupil who was called Anneliese, who had profound multiple learning difficulties and loved *Coronation Street*. We asked permission for her to come to the location and her mum and Helen arrived with her during our lunch break. She was treated like a queen, and had photographs taken with every member of the cast. She particularly responded to voices and squealed with delight when she heard Jimmy Harkishin who plays Dev, and Simon who played Steve.

Anneliese is in her early twenties and Helen taught her ten years previously but had kept in touch. The actors were delighted to oblige, and Anneliese's mum told us later that she was so happy to have met them. Most of the Corrie people do their share of charitable work. There are always cast photographs in the green room to be signed, and the notice board is always full of requests. They will generally do what they can – often unheralded – with work schedules which are demanding. Most realise that they are in a very fortunate position and will try to give something back.

During the three weeks between filming and transmission, I was approached several times to see if I would 'spill the beans' and was interviewed on *Radio Five Live* to try to get some information about the wedding, but I kept quiet. It really is amazing, the hold that Corrie has on some people and more than once I have been asked if I am really a vicar, and where is my church?

During the filming of the wedding, I noticed David Neilson who plays Roy Cropper sitting quietly in a pew doing *The Times* crossword. Some members of the regular cast are not too fond of big storylines like weddings and bring stuff to read to keep the boredom at bay. I respected David's privacy and did not approach him. A few weeks later, Helen and I were at Oldham to see a new play. The real-life husband of Julie Hesmondhalgh, who plays Roy's wife Hayley in the show, had written it. David and his wife had gone to see it to support him. In the bar before the show, David came over and said, "hi Jim, your stuff is on next week." I was well chuffed that he had spoken, and we sat together afterwards. David's wife had taught children with special needs and so she and Helen had a good old chat and David told us that he was returning to the stage for a short time to play in *Waiting for Godot* at the Library theatre in Manchester. We went to see it and he was brilliant.

David was very friendly with Pete Postlethwaite and he came to see the play the same evening. We were all having a chat in the bar afterwards and I told Pete how much I had enjoyed his portrayal of Prospero at the Royal Exchange. He thanked me and said, "I went on the Simon Mayo show you know and some chap phoned and said he had tears in his eyes, and sand in his toes, we sold loads more tickets after that."

I did not have the nerve to say that it was me, but isn't it ironic that I'm selling tickets for them, and they won't employ me?

Outside the permanent set in the centre of Manchester, there are always fans who wait all day to try and get autographs or photos with the cast. One chap has been standing outside just waiting for the stars for many years. All the regulars have stopped and given him the time of day at some point. After my last recording session at Stage One, I was leaving in my car when he jumped in front of me. I wound down the window and said, "I don't think you want me mate."

"Yes, I do Jim, I know who you are. You're the Vicar, can I have a photo with you?"

For me to be recognised was unheard of, so I pulled in to let him take the photo.

Just then a voice said, "Hello Jim, are you OK?" It was David. The chap immediately gave him the camera and told him to take a picture of us. David laughed and said, "I bet you get this all the time Jim."

We were in the ridiculous position of one of the most recognised faces in the country taking my photograph with one of my 'fans'. Very satisfying. Hee hee!

32: Bus Driving

Next, came an audition at Yorkshire TV, for a vicar in *Emmerdale*. Granada and Yorkshire have been the same company for years, and some of the executive producers have worked on both *Coronation Street* and *Emmerdale*, so I thought that as I had just played a vicar in Corrie, in a high profile plotline, I would have no chance. Perhaps I should have remembered my unhappy 'Grimble' experience at YTV and shouldn't have been so surprised when I got the job.

The plot was once again quite high profile, dealing with the wedding of Patsy Kensit's character to her rich fiancée Alisdair, but true to nearly all of the weddings at which I had officiated, the wedding was disrupted.

Sadie's 'true love' Matthew King came running into the church and 'Sadie' ran away with him before the ceremony had ended. One thing that should be said about *Emmerdale* is that from a guest actor's point of view, it is the friendliest soap to do. There is one actor who makes a point of welcoming any new face appearing on the set. Chris Chittell, who plays villainous Eric Pollard, always introduces himself, and makes you feel at home. This makes a tremendous difference to nervous first timers and is much appreciated.

I decided that the time had come to give up taxi driving. The job had become more and more dangerous from my point of view and I had crashed the taxi in a manoeuvre, which, although not my fault, brought home to me that I was not getting any younger. I was sick to death of rising at 4.00am that, of course, meant going to bed at nine. One thing for sure, I would not have been able to manage it if I was still drinking. Taxi drivers were used to driving ten- or twelve-hour shifts, there were no safeguards to curtail the long hours, no tacographs in the cab and it was no job for someone approaching sixty.

Andrew and Lucy had both graduated by now and were no longer reliant on us and Helen had just a couple of years to go until retirement. My work ethic was such that I couldn't just sit at home doing nothing, and after chatting to a mate, I took my PSV driving test to drive for a company taking children with special needs to school in the mornings and home in the afternoon. My first morning I met Janet the escort, and we set off for the kids. Our children had some language difficulties, but apart from that were perfectly normal. They were cheeky, and very engaging. They kept us in our place, and I became very attached to them.

Our last pick-up before school was a little boy called Declan, who was in floods of tears. He was frightened of his first day at school as he was only four years old. We made a fuss of him and for the second day, I made him a badge that said, 'first bus driver's assistant'. He sat on the little seat behind me and next to Janet and copied me as I changed gears. Within a week, he was running to the bus in the mornings. Of course I remembered my early days at school and was happy for him.

The opposite end of the spectrum from Declan was Ryan. Ryan was only five but had an answer for everything and Janet and I very rarely had the last word. He appeared to have a terrific sense of humour, and what made him even funnier was the fact that he didn't really know what he was saying. One morning before Ryan got on board, the other kids were having a deep discussion about pregnancy, and the oldest boy was pretending to be an expectant mother. As he came up the steps, Ryan summed up the situation in a second and said about the big boy, "what's up with him?"

Someone else said, "she's having a baby and she's in a lot of pain, what can we do?"

Ryan said, "Give her some cake."

For two years, I derived a terrific amount of pleasure from this job. The kids were singularly unimpressed by seeing me on telly but were really full of admiration for the way I drove the bus.

33: The Royle Family

One day as I was picking up my bus from the depot, Elizabeth rang. I pulled in to take the call. "Hello darling, where are you?"

I told her and said that I would be home at 4.45pm.

"OK love, this is what's happening. We've had a call from *The Royle Family*. They're looking for someone to play an Irish priest. They have seen a few but none were right, so I'm going to give you a phone number to ring when you get home and call me later. Meanwhile practice your Irish accent."

Wow! I had never been auditioned over the phone before. All the way round I was mumbling to myself in an Irish accent. The kids must have thought I'd finally snapped.

When I arrived home, I phoned my agent, she gave me a number and said, "Caroline Aherne is waiting for you to call. Please destroy the number when you have finished, as it is her home phone. Oh, and Craig Cash will be there as well."

I was now trembling as I dialled, and Caroline answered.

"Hiya Jim, I'm sorry to ask you to do this over the phone, but we like your photo, you seem to be just what we want but we must have a genuine accent so when I say go, just spout away."

As part of my cabaret act, I used to tell Irish stories, so I just launched into it. After about a minute of this diatribe, Caroline shouted "OK Jim, you can shurrup now, you've got the job. You are Father Kennedy."

Craig shouted from the background, "you'll be ordained on Wednesday." I muttered grovelling thanks and rang off.

When you are not working, it seems as though nobody wants to speak to you, but as soon as you get a job, the phone starts to ring. Firstly, Elizabeth rang to confirm the booking, and then Granada called to tell me that the read through was at the Groucho club in London. Next came calls from wardrobe, make-up and various production people from the BBC. I could hardly believe that I was to be part of one of the greatest television programmes of the last ten years. Even my accountant Eileen Little rang to say that her son Ralf called and said, with some excitement, "Hey mum, guess who's playing the Irish priest in our next *Royle*? Jim Whelan."

Then my insecurity started to kick in, would I survive the read through?

On the day of the read-through, a Saturday, I was on the early train to London. As usual, I had hardly slept since receiving the script. Father Kennedy was a nice little part, but my paranoia knew no bounds. Would they accept my accent? No one had met me yet, would they think I didn't look right for the part? Why couldn't I just relax and enjoy the moment?

The read through as usual, was packed with actors, casting directors, accountants, wardrobe and make-up people. Ralf greeted me with a cuddle. I was overwhelmed and overawed but tried not to show it. We started to read the show, which was a one hour special, and it became clear that the genius of this programme was a combination of writing, which allowed actors to say their lines as if they were sitting next to the viewer, and characterizations which were brilliant from people like Ricky Tomlinson, Sue Johnson, and especially Liz Smith as Nana. Several times we had to stop because people were laughing so much, and I thought to myself that, *if half of this comedy transfers to the screen, it will be sensational.* After the read-through, we all chatted for a while and I shared a cab back to Euston with the lovely June West, the casting director from Granada. They were making the programme at their Manchester studios for the BBC.

There were two weeks to wait before filming. I waited with trepidation for something to go wrong, what was the matter with me? The following week a new script arrived and I saw that Father Kennedy had been given some extra dialogue, so it seemed that I was OK, but still I couldn't relax because I was so happy to be involved in such a big programme. If something had gone wrong then, I do not know what I would have done. Why no confidence? Ah well I have always been like this.

The day of my filming arrived. I was in my usual state when I signed in at Granada studios. After being shown to my dressing room, I asked to see the set so that I could acclimatise myself. We were in the giant Studio Six, which was where I filmed my first Corrie so many years before. The production staff and technicians looked exhausted, not surprising really, as they had just worked fifteen, twelve-hour days, with only one day off in the middle.

We had the final two days to shoot a very complicated and dramatic last scene in the show. It included dialogue from ten or so characters, loads of live music and singing and, just to make it more difficult, the mood changed quite markedly during the scene.

After five hours wait, I was called to the set for a rehearsal. Caroline and the director Mark Mylod said hello. Craig Cash and Phil Mealy, the other two writers, were watching on monitors. My first segment seemed to go well and we went for a 'take.'

If you thought rationally about it, you would never do this job. There are fifty or so 'techies', writers, wardrobe, make-up and sundry other people just concentrating on you. In theory, you should just block them out and concentrate. This I managed to do and was reasonably happy with the result. I should have known better.

Caroline came on to the set. "Aw Jim when we wrote this, we had no idea that you would make it so funny and so real, but could you just try and do it like this?"

This hurt after thinking the first take was OK, but my co-actor in this segment, my old mate Peter Martin of Unigate milkman fame, said, "Just listen to Caroline and do what she says because she's always right."

I did and the improvement was amazing. I decided to go with the flow from then on. Thinking about it later, I tried to figure out what it is that makes the difference between us ordinary performers and people like Caroline who can write, act, and most importantly keep the whole picture in their head and direct the whole shooting match? I do not know, but to me it's sheer genius.

The scene evolved over the two days, and finally we 'wrapped' at 11 o'clock. We decamped to the posh V&A Hotel next door to the studios, for a right royal booze-up. I was so tired that I could hardly see straight, and as I was not drinking anyway, I stayed for an hour and left.

When it was all over, I realised that I had been involved in possibly the most Iconic programme of the last ten years. I worked with people of the calibre of Sue Johnson, Ricky Tomlinson, Liz Smith, Jessica Stevenson and Craig Cash, who co-wrote it with Caroline and Phil Mealy. Heady days!

Now that it was finished, I wondered why I was worried, and vowed to enjoy myself more next time, or perhaps that was just a pipe dream?

Three months later, I received a call from John Rushton, the producer. "Jim I just wanted to ring you to say that due to the fact that we have overrun on the filming of the programme, your dialogue has had to be cut. I just wanted you to know that this is in no way a reflection of your performance and is simply because of time constraints."

It was nice of him to ring me personally and was much appreciated.

Me, paranoid? Hmmm.

34: Training Doctors

Next, was a part in an American film shooting in Liverpool. The film was to be called *Digital Jesus,* and was about a serial killer who was bumping people off 'live 'so to speak on the Internet and, of course, taunting the police.

My role was as a victim, and my 'dialogue' consisted mainly of pleading for mercy, before having my head blown off. The technique of how it was shot fascinated me. They filmed my 'speeches', and carefully locked the film camera in place, and replaced me with a dummy. Then a real shotgun appeared and after starting the camera, my 'head' was blown off. It was a realistic likeness of me, and it gave me a shivery feeling to see myself blasted to death.

The star was Armand Assante and to me he seemed a bit po-faced, but one of the make-up girls told me that he was quite nice really, but daren't smile because he was full of Botox, being too old for the character he was playing. From the scuttlebutt on set, and the arguments all around, the film never seemed to have much of a chance and went straight to video with a change of title to *Dot.Kill.*

I discovered a new source of income round about this time. One of the actors on *Emmerdale* had told me that they did something called 'simulated patient' work for various medical schools. This sounded interesting and so I applied. After attending a couple of workshops and acclimatisation days to tell me what it was all about, I did my first paid job. The university would send a scenario to the actor, who would learn it. On the day, medical students who would attempt to 'diagnose' the patient's condition in ten minutes in an exam situation would interview the 'patient'.

The students were usually trembling. This was a nerve-wracking time for them. It was also not an easy option for the actor, who could only answer according to questions put to him by the student. The temptation is always to be helpful and lenient, but this could lead to unsuitable or unready people getting through, so the temptation is to be avoided.

I, of course, had the advantage of being able to ring Andrew and discuss the scenarios with him. Simulated patients are an exceedingly small part of the examination systems for trainee doctors and their input is minuscule in the overall scheme of things. The money is not particularly generous, but it still gives a lot of satisfaction. When my badminton cronies ask why I am not available on a certain day, I tell them that I'm training doctors.

One ambition, which I never came near to realising, was to work with Mike Leigh. I have always been a great admirer of his work and he seems to elicit wonderful performances from his actors. Mike is the same age as I am and was born and lived around the corner in the better off Jewish area. He went to Grecian St School, not far from us in Higher Broughton and, for all I know, I could have been his family's 'Shabbos goy'. We used to pass his Dad's surgery every morning on our way to School. We of course inhabited different, if parallel Universes, and still do.

His method of working fascinates me, starting with one-to-one discussions with the actors, and building up a 'back story' of how the character has developed. This is before a script has even evolved. He gets unswerving loyalty and commitment from actors, and it shows in the gritty and truthful portrayals from such luminaries as Timothy Spall, and Alison Steadman.

You would think he might like to meet me, and chew the fat about the 'old days', but despite my repeated letters to his office, he shows a marked reluctance. He probably thinks I'm a stalker. Does the man not realise that I have appeared in Sooty?

35: Rogue Traders, Moving On

After what seemed a long time without work, I got a call from Elizabeth to go to Liverpool for an audition. LA Productions were shooting the third series of a daytime series called Moving On. Jimmy McGovern was involved, and anything that carries his name is worthwhile. She told me that Michelle Smith, who was the Casting Director, did not think I looked ancient enough to play the character who is an old man, so I decided to go unshaven and scruffy. When Michelle saw me, she asked if I was feeling all right. So, my two-day's growth and tatty appearance was working.

The director asked me to read the part and when I had finished, just said, "Well, nothing more to say, thanks for coming Jim".

I drove home wondering if he meant that I had done well, or did he just want this dirty apparition out of his sight?

It must have been the former because I got the job, my scenes were with Reece Dinsdale, late of 'Corrie' and the shoot was in a week, plenty of time to learn my lines.

The day before the shoot, Elizabeth told me to get myself down to the BBC in Manchester to meet someone from Rogue Traders. I hadn't a clue what they wanted, but there was no harm in going.

I met Nicole, a nice young girl who asked me to act out a scenario pretending that I was a harmless old man, and a 'bent' plumber was ripping me off. I liked role-play. My experience with the medical simulations meant that I was in practice and they seemed rather impressed that I had been part of the Noel Edmonds Hit Squad all those years ago. I also by now had a week's growth; must have looked every inch the poor old chap.

I forgot about this job and went to Liverpool to meet up with Reece and film our parts. Everything went well, and we got the scenes in the can. As we rehearsed my main scene, Reece gave me some advice about 'underplaying' some of my responses. This was another instance of a younger, but vastly more experienced actor helping me out. He was right, and I was so grateful. The only awkward thing for me was keeping quiet on the catering bus as Paul Usher, who was co starring with Reece and had played Barry Grant on Brookside for so many years, held forth about the sorry state of Liverpool FC. As a United fan, I thought discretion was the better course.

My filming finished about three pm, and when I switched on my phone, which of course was off during filming, I had four missed calls and a message to ring my agent urgently. I spoke to Elizabeth and she told me that I had got the Rogue Traders job and they were coming to my house at four, to film me making some calls. Thankfully the M62 was fairly traffic free and I arrived home to see a cameraman unloading his car and Nicole, who I had met at the interview. They explained that I had to make two calls to 'Rogues', giving an address in Penrith, Cumbria: one concerning a faulty computer and the other to do with a damp proof firm who were conning people into having cavity wall insulation which was not needed. These calls had to be recorded for legal reasons, the BBC of course having to be seen to be above reproach. The first call was successful, and the man agreed to come and look at the computer at the address in Penrith. The second call proved less so. They said that their Cumbria rep was off ill, and they could not do anything in that area at the moment. It was now Thursday, and the Traders team drove back to London to re-think their strategy. I got a call the following day and was booked to go to Penrith for the whole of the following week.

Hannah from the Rogue Traders team called for me, and we set out for Cumbria. She was delightfully chatty and regaled me with stories of how wonderful it was and how they were one big happy family. She also told me that the damp proof company had been called by a researcher claiming to be my daughter and said that they could come and inspect another house, this time near Nottingham on Thursday. I was to telephone them later in the week to confirm. As we travelled, it became clear that my part as the innocent dupe was the culmination of up to three months work. A knot started to form in my stomach. Although I was confident that I could carry off the old man scenario, it was not going to be a stroll.

The director Jon met us at the house they had rented. Also, in attendance were a 'hidden camera' person, a sound engineer and two further researchers. Jon lost no time in filling me in on what was required. I was to be fitted with a special shirt, which had a camera in a button as well as a microphone. Around my waist was a belt containing power packs, and in my ear was a 'fizzywinkle'. This looked like a hearing aid and allowed the director to speak to me without the 'Rogue' hearing. We had agreed that the culprit was to come and look at my laptop the following day. This had been given a virus, by an expert in London, which should be easy to remove on the spot. There was also a desktop that was running slowly and I was to ask him about this.

The George Hotel in the centre of Penrith was my 'digs'; I was dropped off and tried to get some sleep. My mind was working overtime and sleep wouldn't come. I realised that I was well out of my comfort zone. The responsibility now seemed immense. Fear of the unknown was, I suppose the reason that kept me awake.

Bright and early Tuesday morning, I was picked up and taken to the house. In the upstairs lounge where the computers were to be examined, there were four hidden cameras. Other cameras covered the entrance, stairs, and kitchen, and a nondescript van out in the street contained another camera person to record the arrival and departure.

Yet again it was drummed into me that at no time was I to try to 'lead' the person, the theory was that I was to let him speak in the hope that he would compromise himself. The man was known in the area as a tricky customer, who took money from ordinary people, whilst not doing the work he had promised, and indeed, was often not needed.

On many occasions, he would try to sell people 'new' computers, which contained used and clapped out parts. Trading Standards had a list of complaints going back five years but had never managed to obtain enough evidence to prosecute.

The 'Rogue' was to come at 12.00, but we were to be ready at 11.00, and then came what the team called lockdown. The Rogues, by their very nature were unreliable and we had to be there in plenty of time with everything in place. If, as often happened, they came early, we had to be prepared. My camera was checked, my 'fizzywinkle' inserted and we settled down to wait.

To try to describe that last hour makes me sound like a paranoid worrier. I was convinced that I looked like a Michelin man, with a belt round my waist, a hidden camera in my shirt and a 'fizzywinkle' in my ear. I tried to seem normal, sitting on the settee reading the paper, but my stomach was churning. Jon's instructions were going through my mind and fear of the unknown was making me feel panicky, I could not even go for a pee because I was aware that my every sound was being recorded.

After what seemed like a week, my earpiece spoke, "here he comes, everyone ready".

I waited until a bang came on the door and went downstairs. The man was called John. I asked him to follow me upstairs to the lounge, showed him the laptop, and told him that although I knew nothing about computers, I was lost without it.

He spent ten minutes putting DVDs in and told me that he couldn't do anything there and then but would have to take it away. He said that it would cost £110 to repair. I demurred a little but agreed. He then asked about the desktop, which I said belonged to my stepson. After examining it, he said he could take it away and put a new hard drive-in for £50. I reluctantly agreed to this and he packed them both up. He told us that he would bring them both back on Friday at 11.00am and left.

As his car disappeared up the road, everyone breathed again. Jon was happy with my 'performance 'and we could relax.

Jon asked one of the runners to go to Morrison's in Penrith, to get a chicken and some veg. He decided that as we had the rest of the day off, he would make us a chicken dinner. This was a first, being cooked for by a senior BBC person. They also obtained wine and soft drinks and we had a lovely evening. The food was great, and I got to know people better. It really did seem that there was a family atmosphere, and it was clear that we were all in this together. The team knew each other from previous jobs, but I as the newcomer, was made welcome.

I slept a little better that night and the following morning Jon set up the camera to record my call to the damp proofing firm. This was a National company and the proud boast of the managing director was "I could find damp in the f* * *g Sahara".

A lady answered, saying "Cathedral Damp." Their headquarters were in Derby, but they were a National firm, having surveyors in all areas and sending teams out to complete the work. The woman, when I gave my (false) name said, "Oh Mr Curtis, I was just going to ring you, our managing director will be coming personally to your house tomorrow, as we are so busy".

I thanked her and said that I would expect him at 12.00. Jon and the team were cock-a-hoop at the news, not expecting to get the man himself on film, I was happy for them, but the butterflies had begun.

Thursday, we were up at five am, and on the road from Cumbria to Nottingham. The rush hour traffic was grim on the M1 and we didn't arrive 'till 9 o clock. Setting up commenced and just before eleven, lockdown. Once again, the time dragged interminably, until just before 12, there came a knock on the door.

The man who entered was burly and brusque, but friendly enough. He went around the house and told me I had damp and said that it would cost £1200 to inject foam into the walls to cure the problem. Jon whispered in my ear to ask him what would happen if I didn't get the work done. He said it would cause untold trouble in the future and tried to sell me a vent to go through the wall of the room with the most problems – a mere £270 extra.

To be fair, when I said I would think about it, he did not pressurise me, but left warning me not to leave it too long. Of course, experts had chosen the house because it had no damp whatsoever.

We packed up and set off for Penrith. Arriving at 8.00pm, I collapsed gratefully into bed.

Friday morning back at the house for our final day, we were set up and in lockdown by 10 am. At 10.45, the phone that we used for John rang, the camera was switched on and I answered.

He said, "My car is broken, and I can't come with the computers, I'll bring them tomorrow."

Jon shook his head behind the camera and I had to think quickly. "I won't be here. I'm away at my daughter's for the weekend".

John then said he would bring them on Tuesday and hung up. We had a conference. It was impossible to assemble everybody to return next week and the cost would be prohibitive. I phoned him back; "John, I must have my laptop back before I go to my daughter's, get a taxi down and I will pay".

He agreed and we recommenced lockdown. In the rush, we forgot to lock the front door and after 15 minutes, a booming voice shouted, "Hello," and he was halfway up the stairs. People dived into spare bedrooms and I stalled him by saying that I had dozed off. He showed me the computers, I paid him, and he left.

The computers were taken to London and I was dropped off at home. Never had I been so glad to see my own bed and Helen. It was a fascinating week but a frightening one. No one would have blamed me if anything went wrong, but the responsibility weighed heavily. If something is not right in a TV drama, you re-shoot. Here, we had only one chance.

36: Vagabonds

Two weeks later, I was at home when the phone rang.

"Hello Jim, this is Michelle Cox from Rogue Traders. Jon Hunt has told me how wonderful you were on his shoot." (This is actor speak for, you were adequate). "I wondered if you were available to do one for me next week?"

I checked my empty diary, and tried to sound cool and detached, as I agreed to go to Abingdon in Oxfordshire for three days the following week.

Meeting Michelle and the team when I arrived, it was clear that she was very pregnant – seven months in fact – but she was brisk and business-like as she briefed me.

Our 'Rogue,' was a tree person and had a string of complaints against him including threatening old people, vastly overcharging for shoddy work and even marching one pensioner to the cashpoint to get more money.

I made the call and asked if someone could come and look at my garden the following day. Jason said that he was in Bristol and couldn't get there till 1pm. I agreed.

The following morning, we had a bit of a lie-in and arrived at the house, intending to lockdown at 12 o'clock for Jason's arrival. Technicians were all over the place, including the garden when Jason suddenly appeared at 10.30.

A desperate panic ensued. We thought he must have seen everything, and I was pushed out to meet him.

"Oh, I'm sorry mate but I've changed all my arrangements because you said you were coming at one, I'm off to the doctors."

"Yeah, I happened to be in the area, so I came early".

Just then Michelle came out of the house, "come on Dad, we've got to get to the doctors".

I asked Jason if he could come back in an hour. He agreed and drove off. We finished rigging, and I was fitted with the shirt with camera button, microphone and fizzywinkle.

I was convinced that he would not come back but an hour later, he appeared.

I let him in at the rear of the garden, telling him that my daughter was really bossy and had called out the local garage for me to start my car as I had left the lights on and flattened the battery.

We strolled around the garden and I pointed out a couple of trees about fifteen feet high, and asked him how much it would cost to remove them. He said £500, treble the amount it should have cost. I agreed, and he said he would do them the same day.

It was not until he backed his truck in, we saw there were two other people with him, both female: one in her twenties and the other, middle aged. It turned out that they were his wife and mother-in-Law. As he cut the trees, they cleared away.

I went back into the house, trying without success to relax. I could hear James our tree expert passing comment from an upstairs bedroom.

Jason had broken every safety rule in the book, not having any safety equipment. His chainsaw looked on its last legs, the belt coming off at regular intervals. The language was choice, but they worked hard enough. After three hours, my earpiece warned me, he was heading for the house.

I met him and we walked back up the garden and I asked him about prices for some more work. He looked at the things I pointed out and quoted as follows:

Cutting down two smaller trees £400.

Cleaning up a large weeping willow £500.

Cutting a long Leylandi type hedge £700.

This meant that including the work that he had already done, I would owe him £2100. He said that he would do it for £2000.

Reluctantly agreeing, I said that I would go to the bank that afternoon to get cash. He said that he would return tomorrow at 11 am.

The team were happy that the 'doorstep' with Matt and Dan could take place in the morning. Things were set in motion.

We were taking no chances and were at the house at 6.30 am the next morning, Matt arrived and said hello. He took the brief from Michelle and quickly read it, asking some pertinent questions, he is the face of Rogue Traders and must be seen to be completely above board. He expressed the opinion that the scam was not particularly dreadful, and it could be argued from the 'Rogues' point of view, that he was simply carrying out work as quoted for, despite the overcharging. However, when he had seen the dossier on Jason's previous activities, his fears were allayed, and the 'doorstep' set up.

Four security men arrived and assessed the situation. They were led by Shaun, not a man to be trifled with, having a military (SAS) background. He gave us various scenarios and told us in no uncertain terms that nothing would go ahead unless he could absolutely guarantee everyone's safety.

This was now beginning to resemble a military operation. The tension was starting to ratchet up. I was fitted with my body rig, and the bodyguard assigned to me told me that he would always keep me in sight and would never be more than seven seconds from me in case of disaster. My job would be to meet Jason in the garden and lead him to a pre-arranged spot for Matt to leap out.

Lockdown started at 10am and everything went quiet.

We were twelve people in a confined space, all of us waiting for something to happen.

'Rogues' are notoriously unreliable and sure enough at 10.30, one of the lookouts in a car down the lane, crackled over his 'walkie-talkie' to Shaun, "here they come".

Everybody got ready. My heart was going like a hammer.

Shaun suddenly barked, "quiet." His other lookout told him that there was another vehicle, a land rover containing two burly men.

The decision was now Shaun's. He said in a whisper, that he could no longer guarantee safety, especially as two of his men were no longer on the property and the 'doorstep' was aborted.

Jason came around the house shouting "Mr Curtis" and banging on the doors.

We were now in trouble and after a whispered conversation, it was agreed that I should phone him with a story to get rid of them. I went with Michelle to a part of the house we hoped was remote enough for him not to hear me and dialled.

"Hello Jason, I've had a fall and I'm in hospital. I'm sorry but you'll have to leave it for today. I won't let anyone work on my property when I'm not there. I'll phone you later about the money I owe you".

He was not happy, but eventually acquiesced and after some industrial language and shrugging of shoulders, they drove away.

The feeling was of slight relief, but overwhelming disappointment, having been so near to the culmination of up to three months work. Michelle phoned London, and after consulting lawyers, they phoned back in some agitation.

We were now in the worst possible position. The situation had to be resolved because the owners of the house were now in danger of reprisals. There was an angry man who was owed £500 for work already done. He could return at any time and we were responsible. Something had to be done. Further calls to London took place and Matt came up with the only feasible plan. I was to phone Jason and tell him that I would send my son-in-law to the house with the money, and could he come back?

The acting gods must have been with me, or more likely Jason's greed got the better of him. He said he would return in an hour.

I was now out of the equation, being ostensibly in Hospital, but I was feeling the tension as much as anybody.

After an hour, the truck was spotted, but thankfully not the Land Rover. The doorbell rang and Matt, two cameramen, sound people and the security team, exploded out of the door to confront Jason.

He ran for the truck shouting, "It's Rogue Trader, look there's Matt Damon".

There was no whooping or hollering. We realised we had been incredibly lucky. We now had to get out of there as quickly as possible. My security man escorted me to my car, and we all met up back at the hotel.

We had a quick debrief. As the adrenaline evaporated, a feeling of deflation overwhelmed me and I trundled home.

Turning it over in my mind a few days later, I realised that in the final showdown, Jason was outnumbered and for a split second, it was possible to feel sorry for him. But what we had to remember is that for years, he had been mercilessly targeting old and vulnerable people and swindling them out of their hard-earned cash.

37: Meadow Vale

A welcome call came from Elizabeth, telling me to expect a call from the BBC. Rogue Traders.

The call was an hour later from a new name to me, Tom, a producer. They had been trying for some time to get someone from a company who sold pseudo-Medicare products at vastly inflated prices, using mumbo jumbo to baffle older people to part with cash in exchange for products which did little good. Tom told me that a 'sting' had been carried out two weeks previously, but they had elicited little info that would help to trap these people, so he wanted me to try. It was quite delicate, as the firm's method was to cold call people to get appointments. They were always suspicious of people calling them.

An assistant producer, Ceri, was despatched from London, and I picked her up at the station and brought her to my home. We tried a few times to contact Meadowvale, but always got the answerphone. We left messages and Ceri had lunch with us and settled down to wait for a reply.

The special phone which Ceri brought with her, and on which we made the calls, suddenly jangled three hours later. Adopting my 'old fogey' persona, I answered. The lady, after making some enquiries, seemed satisfied that I was 'genuinely' a person suffering rheumatoid arthritis, and various other older person's complaints as per the brief made up by experts, and we made an appointment for three days later. She told me that Russell O* * *would visit me, and that he was one of their top 'Medical Advisors'. In fairness, she did not say that he had had any medical training.

I kept the 'rogue' phone with me, and on the day before our 'sting', the firm rang me to confirm that their advisor would be with me at 1.30 tomorrow. As the appointment was for the afternoon, I travelled on the morning of our operation, arriving in plenty of time to meet Tom and for him to brief me. The best we could hope for was that the rep would commit himself to improper medical claims to sell me the products. We had lockdown at 12 noon, and we settled down. The afternoon dragged interminably, 1.30 passed 2.30 came, we phoned but got only an answerphone. We left messages, but no response. At 4.30, we stood down and tried one more time to ring. Some thought that there was a distinct possibility we had been rumbled. Eventually, they answered and were very apologetic. Russell had had a family emergency, and had to take his teenage son to hospital. Could they come the following week?

Ceri thought that the morning was a much better time to meet as the rep was much less likely to get side-tracked by earlier appointments so we booked for 10.30 am, a week later.

We all travelled down the night before and stayed in a hotel. The next morning, we were at the house very early and lockdown commenced at 9.15 am.

At 10.30 on the dot, an estate car pulled up, and a man came to the door and rang the bell. I took my time answering as befits an infirm old man. Russell O* * *who was about sixty years old, shook my hand, commented that he had the same carpet as me in his house, and settled down.

He stayed for three and a half hours!

To say that time dragged, would be an understatement. Russell proceeded to tell me all about himself, how his first marriage had failed, how many cars he had owned throughout his life, how his working career had taken him around the world, how he had remarried happily, how he had teenage children, how he had ended up being the area and training manager for this company. I tried to interject now and again, but it was really a monologue.

After an hour, Russell said that he would demonstrate the benefits of one of his company's products. He went to his car, and brought in a small mattress, which he unrolled on the bed and plugged in. Taking my shoes off, I lay on it and for the next forty minutes he ran the gamut of the hand control, which when pressed caused differing types of vibration. Some went buzz, some went whirr, and some went whizz. Every now and then he would say, "How does that feel?"

I said it felt different.

"There you are" said Russell. "That proves that it's getting rid of your pain and making your rheumatism better".

The next claim nearly made me laugh out loud. "This oscillation will simulate exercise, and will give as much benefit to you as going for a long walk". He carried on interminably in this vein and when he finally left, I had paid a deposit of £200 on a new mattress, which retailed to me at just under £2.000.

When his car disappeared up the road, the team burst out from the hide, to go to the toilet, and in a couple of cases to have a fag. I remarked that I had done summer seasons that were shorter than that appointment. It had been very difficult to keep concentration for such a long time, and there had been the constant worry that Russell might have seen some evidence of belts, microphones and hidden cameras inside my shirt when I lay on the bed. Some poor person at the BBC would have the unenviable job of transposing the full three and a half hours of dialogue and having it committed to print to be examined by the legal people and medical experts. We were fairly sure that Russell had made some pretty outlandish claims for his vibrating mattress. I couldn't remember all of them, let's wait and see. He also made great play of introducing some more of the company's products, such as armchairs with vibrators in them for up to £3.000, and mobility scooters, which were even more expensive.

We went our separate ways and I heard no more until Tom rang three days later to ask if Ceri could come and film me cancelling the mattress.

This we did, and the attitude of the company changed completely. They said that there were 'procedures' to go through before they could refund, despite the fact that during our meeting, Russell had laid great store by assuring me that if I wanted out of the contract within the statutory seven days, I would get my refund immediately.

After a further week, Tom asked me to phone to set up a final meeting so that Matt could 'doorstep' Russell. They agreed after I told them that I was sorry, perhaps I did want to buy after all, and might also be interested in discussing a chair or a mobility scooter.

There was a moral conundrum here. I was lying to the company and to Russell. There was not a chance that I would have any more dealings with them, and I just wanted to get them to the location so that they could be approached by Matt, and exposed on national television. I had slight misgivings, but I remembered that this company targeted old people, sold them stuff at vastly inflated prices, promising them health benefits which didn't exist, and had been doing so for many years.

It was a tense weekend for me. I had the 'rogue' phone in my possession and had to wait until Monday for the firm to confirm that Russell will come on Tuesday. On Monday morning, I was like a cat on hot bricks, jumping at every sound whilst waiting for them to ring. If they didn't call by 12.30pm, I would have to contact them. This I hated doing because I felt it was arousing suspicion. At 11.45am, I decided that I had better have my shower, and then call Tom for instructions. The phone rang as I was drying myself, and adopting my helpless old man persona, I answered. They confirmed that they would see me tomorrow at 10.30am, and with great relief, I rang Tom. He sounded as happy as me, and things swung into motion.

We stayed in the hotel again and rose early the next morning. I said hello to Matt Allwright at breakfast. I feel that Matt's success as a broadcaster is that he is completely genuine, he never patronises, and I always feel at home in his company. We arrived at the house at 8am and discussed the format of the 'doorstep'. My job is relatively easy this time, all I have to do is greet Russell and send him in front of me into the living room. Matt and I were dressed in sports gear and he was running on a treadmill. The premise being that he can then start his piece to Russell by saying "now that is exercise, not lying on a mattress being vibrated", thus showing up the claims of the benefits of the highly priced bed.

Nearly always, the 'rogue' just turns and makes a sharp exit, but to everyone's surprise Russell was not for leaving and sat down on the settee to argue it out with Matt with a camera crew, sound man and director in full view. He seemed quite put out that Matt should try to impugn his integrity, saying loudly that he only helped people, that he stayed for over three hours because he thought people were lonely, and said quite angrily that "it's about time someone stood up to you lot". He left after more than twenty minutes and before leaving, said that he knew that it would be edited, and they had better not make him look bad or he would denounce them on Twitter.

Having eavesdropped on most of this, I was nonplussed. A breath-taking performance, maybe foolhardy from Russell. He asserted all the time that he was just helping folks, that he wanted to continue doing good, that he was doing the right thing. Either he was completely deluded, or this was his only course of action, having been 'caught' bang to rights' on a three and a half hour film, making clearly outrageous and nonsensical claims for the equipment.

During the rest of the day, Matt and I filmed a sequence of 'funnies'. The idea being, to make a 'Rocky' type montage to illustrate how proper exercise was the only real way to fitness. These little extras are fun to do, and can be either quite amusing, or butt-clenching embarrassing. We shall see. One side effect of them is that it ups my profile. This is something I have tried to avoid as I love doing Rogues, but if I am recognised on a sting, I will be finished.

Home now, and time to think. I miss the buzz, especially as this was a difficult one and in total has lasted five weeks for me. I was feeling a bit guilty, as I had been lying to people, so I Googled the company. There were dozens of complaints, from targeting people in their eighties, selling them unsuitable and in some cases harmful products at plainly exorbitant prices. This made me feel that the subterfuge was warranted. We will see how it plays out. It is now the day of the transmission. Should I tell people that it is on?

A week after the programme went out, I watched through my fingers. Looking again a few days later, I am reasonably satisfied. The editing was fair to Russell, and it was plain that he had no real answer to the charges. Even the 'funnies' were not too bad, and the firm must have been slowed in their tracks with the targeting of old people to sell equipment that costs a fortune and does no good.

Six months later I idly Googled the firm, they have gone into liquidation.

38: Sad Coronation Street

Two incredibly sad *Coronation Street* jobs came in the last year.

First was the funeral of Vera Duckworth. The news had been leaked in the press that Liz Dawn was leaving for health reasons. I desperately hoped that I would get the job especially considering my long association both with Liz, and Bill. Of course, the casting department knew nothing of this and as I was not under any sort of contract or retainer, I was in their hands.

It was a great relief when Elizabeth phoned to tell me they wanted me, and I looked forward to working with Bill again. Reading the script, I realised that Bill was due to read a very moving eulogy to his beloved 'swamp duck', and I wondered how he would approach it.

The first assistant director was John Folkard from *Brookside* some years before, so we knew that we were in good hands. Before the take for Jack Duckworth's main speech in the church, he warned the whole cast and crew, especially the younger cast members who were naturally a little more boisterous than the senior actors, that he wanted complete and utter silence.

As the scene unfolded, the vicar after the usual homilies and prayers asked if anyone would like to say anything before the coffin disappeared. At first there was no response, but then Jack decided that he had better say something. As he shuffled towards me at the pulpit, his breathing was wheezy and he took his time.

It was one of those moments that you do not ever forget. Over the years, Jack and Vera had been entwined with all our lives. Their squabbles, their triumph such as when they had a windfall, delivered by me as the postie, which enabled them to take over the Rovers, went through my mind. Their desperate downs with their son Terry, who was in prison, and let out for the day, handcuffed to two prison officers, for Lisa Duckworth's funeral at which I officiated. In a strange way, truth and fantasy merged for me. Bill's delivery of the speech had all of us in tears, and I was relieved that I had nothing to say after that.

Bill has long been a worry to people. He still smokes despite having a heart operation some years ago, and I could not help remembering our first meeting in a seedy club in Bolton. He is such a down to earth person, not at all 'show biz', and I sometimes think that he doesn't realise how much the public loves him, as Jack.

Also, in the congregation of course were Anne Kirkbride and Barbara Knox. I unashamedly showed off photos of my new grandson Ben. I once again thought how long a road it had been since Oldham Rep so many years before.

The second Corrie job was to 'officiate' at the funeral of the stillborn son of Maria and Liam.

Samia Smith, who plays Maria, had seemed to do nothing but cry for the previous 12 months. Liam, who had confessed his love for his sister-in-law Carla, had betrayed her. They had been in turmoil and, to add to everything else, the boy Paul, had been stillborn.

My first scene was with Carla and Liam, where the vicar thinks that Carla is the mother and to everyone's embarrassment, says that he hoped that her sorrow at the loss of her son would soon ease. I loved playing 'proper' bits like this, and Rob James Collier and Alison King were as usual, great with me.

It was a beautiful day, and the unit was in particularly high spirits. The 'techies', cameramen and drivers were having a good-natured argument about the weekend's football. Everyone was in a good mood.

A black estate car drew up, not a hearse, and when the driver opened the tailgate, a small white coffin was revealed. Of course, we all knew it was only make believe, but silence fell. The next couple of hours were as sombre as I can ever remember on the set, and when Rob as Liam carried the tiny coffin containing his 'son', into the church, the whole unit was in bits.

Maria turned up as we were entering the church and she and Liam gave heart-breaking performances.

One of my hobbyhorses about 'soap' acting is that performers are routinely – and in my opinion unfairly – criticised. To give a convincing performance and appear in people's homes six times a week is no mean feat. Many actors, who appear to be fine performers when seen in small roles, can soon be 'found out' when they are on screen for the longer time, which long running series demand. Also, the sheer physical demands of a working pattern which can last up to three weeks without a day off, is very exhausting, no wonder some high-profile names fall by the wayside.

Being constantly in the public eye is not always easy either. I shared a car from the location one day with Jenny McAlpine, who plays Fizz. She is a lovely Bury lass. When I asked her jocularly if she had been out on the razzle that weekend, she told me that she did not like to go out much because of what happened a little time before. In the Coronation Street storyline, she was involved in a romantic situation where she had to choose between two suitors. As she was walking down Market Street in Manchester, a 'wag' shouted, "choose Kirk you fat cow."

If she ignored the jibe, she is a 'stuck up mare', if she remonstrated, she is a 'bad tempered cow who is too big for her boots'.

Her only answer was to smile sweetly and carry on, but to a sensitive person this is very cruel. I remembered from my days with Mike and Bernie, that the public can be spiteful.

I was sharing a caravan with Rob James Collier. The newspapers were full of the story that he was leaving the show. During a long chat, I asked him why. He said that he was afraid of being typecast. He wanted to do something like a programme he had seen a few years before where people were singing and dancing in between the drama. It was a show he thought was great. It was called *Blackpool*.

I thought that he was 'taking the 'mickey', but when I told him that I had been in that, he was amazed, and went around telling everyone. It seemed that *Blackpool* had achieved a sort of iconic status, and I was inordinately proud, even though my involvement had been small.

The writer of *Blackpool* had of course, been Pete Bowker. Sometime after my chat to Rob, I saw that a three-part series was about to be shown called *Occupation*. I watched it and was knocked out. It was an intelligent and superbly acted story of the effects on young soldiers and their families during the conflict in Iraq.

I felt I had to say something to Pete who had written it and dug out a postcard, which he had sent to every member of the Blackpool cast and contained his email. I told him my feelings and mentioned what Rob had said and told him there was no need to reply. The reply came within the hour, and Pete said how pleased he was to hear from me, he was chuffed at Rob's comments, and that whenever I appeared on Corrie, he used to say to his young daughter, "he was in Blackpool you know." The girl used to tell him off for trying to make out that he knew famous actors.

My next visit to the street was to pay a visit to Carla and Tony. The vicar had been asked to come and speak to Carla to try to console her after the death of Liam. Once again, this was a pastoral visit, and I was looking forward to an intimate scene with Gray as Tony and Alison as Carla.

In the green room, I said hello to Gray, and he asked if I minded if we went through the lines. He looked exhausted, and it turned out that he and Alison were just coming to the end of a nineteen-day shooting schedule, including night shoots, which play hell with your body clock.

We tried to rehearse, and it was clear that he did not know his lines. Alison was asleep on the settee on the set, and when she woke and joined us, she did not know her lines either. I was a little perturbed but had no choice but to carry on.

We had two run-throughs and went for a take. They were both perfect with their words. Why had I worried?

Absolute professionalism, time after time.

39: D.I.Y. Baby

I decided that it was time to give up the bus driving. I was in my sixty-fifth year, and although I enjoyed the job, I found it very tying. As I was now doing lots more 'simulated patient work, I felt guilty when I had to tell the firm that I needed time off for my various other activities. We parted on good terms, and I still see some of the other drivers from time to time. When Janet told little Ryan that I was finishing he said, "no offence Jim, but you are pretty old."

It was now October 2010, and Ruth – Andrew's wife – was nine months pregnant.

Andrew had taken three weeks off to look after little Ben and the new arrival, but he showed no signs of hurrying along.

They found out that it was a boy from the scan and had decided on a home birth. Although Andrew is a Doctor, he could not treat Ruth and a midwife was ready at the end of a phone. A birthing pool was borrowed, and all they can do is wait.

At 4.00am, Ruth felt some pangs.

Andrew phoned for the midwife, but she was in the middle of a delivery elsewhere, and not available. The paramedics were despatched, but the baby decided to arrive, and was delivered by Andrew.

When he phoned us, we were assailed by screaming baby cries and a proud dad said that it "looks like a big-un." Indeed, he was, weighing in at 10lbs and a bit.

I know that there are many good reasons why doctors cannot treat their families. Apart from advice, Andrew will not have anything to do with treating Helen and Me, but I cannot help but feel immense pride and love. Whatever have I done to deserve my good fortune? And how cool is that, to deliver your own son?

A couple of days later when we went to prod the newcomer – now named Lucas – I got Andrew on one side and asked if there were any complications and was it like in the western films of my youth when you heard a sharp smack, followed by a loud baby wail?

He said that everything was relatively straightforward, but he felt very alone, whilst trying to reassure Ruth that he knew exactly what he was doing. Apparently, you do not smack the newborn, but gently and firmly rub. This can take up to two minutes, and as the seconds dragged on it seemed an eternity.

When the time arrived and the baby gave a first splutter, in a split second a hole in the heart closed, the child's arteries started carrying the blood through the body under its own steam, and the baby breathed the first breath. Wow!

40: Beach Wedding

Lucy phoned to tell us that Joe had proposed, and they wanted to be married on the lovely little Island of Lankawi, just off the coast of Malaysia, and a quick one-hour flight from Kuala Lumpur.

Helen and I were delighted, we love Joe, he is a caring and kind person with a tremendous Social Conscience, and we were sure that Lucy would be in good hands.

Of course, we travelled to the Island, and were really touched that so many of Lucy and Joe's friends were coming, and several of our own friends from Bury came, treating it as their summer holiday, although it was only March.

The Ceremony was on the beach, but on the morning of the wedding, lots of legal formalities had to be attended to. Bride and groom – with both sets of prospective in laws – ran around to a Solicitor, Notaries, and a Justice of the Peace, before the beach ceremony. All went to plan, and as everybody waited on the Beach at the swanky resort hotel. I escorted my lovely Lucy in a Golf cart down to the seaside, covered seats were set out, and a beautiful arch of flowers was assembled. Something spontaneous happened which we will remember for a long time. Three-year-old Grandson Ben, who was standing near his Mummy and Daddy, just walked to my side and reached for my hand. Lucy smiled at him, and we three walked down the 'Aisle' together.

I joined Helen with Ben in my arms, and we watched a lovely service, with a specially written poem for the couple by Mike, Joe's Dad, which was beautiful.

The resort Hotel had pulled out all the stops, and the food and setting were magnificent for the evening part. My speech, which I had rehearsed that morning walking up and down the beach, went well enough, and it was great to see everyone having such a fine time.

Eighteen months later, Lucy delivered a bouncing, flame headed little boy who they called Thomas, and we went out to Kuala Lumpur to see them within a couple of months. Thomas was and is a bright, inquisitive funny and lovable chap who keeps us constantly entertained.

Lucy and Joe always intended to stay abroad for five years; they returned and started looking for a place to put down roots. Looking around the South Coast, they loved Eastbourne, and decided that this was the place for them and after renting for some months, bought a house there.

41: The End for Me?

My Agent is on Holiday, so I get a call from her assistant Ann.

"Granada ITV want to see you tomorrow morning for the part of Vicar in Coronation Street."

I felt a bit miffed to be honest. After ten years and some twenty plus episodes in some of the biggest storylines in 'The Street', why would they want to audition me?

Of course, I say yes and arrived the following morning at the studios to find four other actors, all of whom I knew, and all of who have played Vicars in 'Corrie'.

We are given the script and one scene stuck out. It was a meeting between Tyrone, Kirsty and the Vicar, and called for some serious acting all round. The Vicar asked Tyrone what Kirsty meant to him, and what this marriage means. He broke down as he tried to explain how his own family meant nothing to him. He did not know what love was, until taken in by Jack and Vera. He said that Jack was a father to him and due to the example of the way that Jack and Vera looked after each other, he would make a true dad to Ruby.

I did my best reading this scene and went home.

The following day Ann called and said that the part was mine, everyone in the casting department said that they were delighted, and the important scene would be emailed to me to shoot two days later.

We shot the scene at St Mary's Prestwich, it seemed to go well, and it was lovely to meet up again with Alan Halsall. Natalie Gumede was a revelation, obviously nothing like the person she plays. She is a sweet and gentle girl, which makes her portrayal of Kirsty even more remarkable. As we left, I said that I hoped to see them again in four weeks for the Wedding scenes. I had not been officially booked and had learned never to take anything for granted.

Ten days later Elizabeth who was back in the office rang with confirmation, what a relief. The scripts arrived, together with the dates and I started learning.

141

What follows mystified me and has shredded my confidence and self-esteem.

Elizabeth called and said, "what I am going to say will upset you, the producer thought that you were too old looking; he is re-casting the Vicar, you will be paid for all the episodes for which you have been booked. I'm so sorry darling, there was nothing I could do".

What will happen to the scene that is already shot? Will they re-shoot? The cost will be enormous, was I that bad? Had fifty years been a delusion? All these thoughts went through my mind and my head was in bits. My friends say, "well at least you got paid" but that is not the point. I felt that I had let everyone down, and at that moment, was at my lowest ebb.

I waited to see what appeared and had to keep saying to myself that this wasn't really important when placed alongside my many blessings such as Helen, Andrew, my grandsons and Lucy, whose baby boy had arrived.

Was I paranoid? Hmm...

Wednesday 4th December – the day of the wedding shoot.

Out of the blue, a lovely message came from Alan Halsall. It said "I am gutted you're not here today, just wanted to let you know that the reason they have had to replace you is because the Church was changed and as you were aligned with the Prestwich one, they had to use another vicar".

This made me feel much better, but if this was the real reason for replacing me, why didn't they say so?

My paranoia continued to niggle at me, why did they say that I was too old?

On Friday 7th December, a large amount of money arrived in my account. I presumed it must have been the 'Corrie' money and made a mental note to find out next week.

I watched the re-shot scene, and was even more mystified. The actor playing the vicar was absolutely fine, very experienced and much more 'well known' than me. The scene itself had been abridged somewhat. Tyrone's input especially seemed much more subdued, perhaps the fact was that Bill Tarmey had died just after the original scene was shot and the producer didn't want to be seen to be playing on it, was the reason?

I was going to be out of the country on the date of the transmission of the wedding scenes. We were going to see Lucy and our lovely new grandson Thomas. I was still feeling bruised. Maybe I will never know the true reason for my sacking?

Eventually, a message came in a roundabout way from a Corrie director who was apparently discussing me with a friend of mine that it was "just one person's opinion". I know who that person was but probably will never meet him.

It was January now, we were all packed up and off to Malaysia to see Lucy, Joe and lovely little Thomas. We would be away for five weeks, and I consoled myself that at least I would not have to watch the wedding scenes.

To an outsider, this might seem an absurdly over the top reaction, and they would be right but I just couldn't get out of my mind that I had been' paid off'.

At my age, I was probably finished with 'The Street' and after nearly fifty years, it wasn't the way I would have chosen to be remembered.

No more chewing the fat with Barbara Knox about weekly Rep or laughing with Ann Kirkbride about her singing of 'Daddy wouldn't buy me a Bow Wow' in the Oldham Rep Music Hall forty years before.

I was gutted.

Ah well…

42: All At Sea

I was invited to audition at Media City, for a children's drama called All at Sea. I must say, it was the best-organised meeting I had attended. Everything ran like clockwork, and we all went in on time. For some reason, I was not nervous and I opened by telling the casting director and director that I had started work here on what used to be Salford Docks. They appeared to be interested, and I even pointed out through the window which building I had worked in as a fifteen-year-old office boy. Of course, I didn't tell them that it was in 1957, because then they would realise how old I was, and I don't think that they would fancy a seventy-two-year-old shopkeeper.

My character had to chastise the kids who were messing around with the gumball machine outside his shop on the front in Scarborough. I called upon my seemingly never-ending games with grandson Ben, in which I pretend to be angry with him for all kinds of imaginary slights. He loves this pretend outrage.

It seemed to go as well as could be hoped. You can never second-guess casting people, so I put it out of my mind.

A week later, I had got the job: one day filming in Scarborough and one around Manchester later in the month.

Helen and I set out to visit Henfield and Eastbourne. We loved visiting Andrew with Ben and Lucas, and then to Lucy and little red headed Thomas.

These days, we find the car journey quite tiring, and wonder how long we can keep it up. We had reached Beaconsfield services and were having sandwiches when Elizabeth calls. "Sorry darling it's sod's law, but they need you in Scarborough on Monday for your first filming day". This meant spending two days at Henfield, driving to Scarborough, and then returning to Lucy's in Eastbourne.

I was not flavour of the month when I set out early on Sunday morning, but I had more to worry about as a nightmare journey of nearly three hundred and fifty miles saw me arriving in Scarborough that evening. Happily, the hotel was fine and I slept well.

The shoot was a joy, no prima donna kids. The director actually gave direction, and the weather was sunny. It is a revelation working with children, and every take had to be one in which they got things right. Some struggled with big words in the dialogue, and now and again a word would be dropped. It is a fine balance between encouraging and flustering them. In this Paul, the director was brilliant, and everything seemed to proceed according to plan. What tickled me was that the two boys just wanted to play football in their down time, just typical young 'uns.

I returned to Eastbourne, again a trip of three hundred and fifty or so miles and we had a lovely time with Lucy and Joe. Thomas is a joy, and we took him to the park etc., but his chief desire was to play in the garden of their new house in a pile of pebbles. He would pick them up, give them to me, and I would surreptitiously put them back. This could go on for some time, and I suspect I would tire first.

This time, the journey home was a nightmare. The M6 was a car park, with every transom showing delays and the journey took two hours longer than usual.

Two weeks later, I turned up for my second day's filming. This time we were at Chorlton High School campus, Manchester. Forty-minute drive, one hour wait, one hour shoot. Finished by 11, home by 12 to sit in the garden, that is more like it.

Happy, happy job loved it!

43: Paranoid, Me? Prey...

I got a call from the office for yet another audition at Beverley Keogh. Anne who rang says that they want to see me for the part of Mr Nutter, a shopkeeper in a drama called From There to Here. This got me rather excited, as I know that the writer was Peter Bowker who wrote Blackpool, one of my happiest memories.

I wonder if perhaps he has remembered and asked for me? When the email arrived, it is for a piece named Prey. I was a little confused as there was a Mr Nutter in it, so it is obviously correct and think I had better ring to avoid confusion. Anne apologised, saying that it was her mistake. She had been casting two things at once and given the wrong name.

The part was a quite nice little vignette; a bit of light comedy set incongruously amongst some very dark goings on and it was starring John Simm, one of my favourite actors.

I tried not to get too excited. I had been to quite a few auditions lately without success, why should this be any different?

The scene was in a garage shop and Mr Nutter (me), was putting tins of Cullen Skink (fish soup), on the shelf and berating his wife for stocking them as he felt that they didn't sell well enough.

I decided for a bit of fun to take a tin with me as a prop. Never having done this before, I felt a bit stupid, but as my success rate had been nil for some time, what had I got to lose?

Beverly Keogh casting was terribly busy, they were casting some commercials, and lots of teenagers for some other drama. David Martin invited me in, explained the scene, and I tried it to camera a couple of times. Back on the street after ten minutes, I was reasonably pleased that I did as well as I could, and now was just determined to put it out of my mind.

Three days later, Anne rang to tell me I was Mr Nutter.

Well fancy that! At last an audition paid off. I Googled the name Prey, and found that the writer was called Chris Lunt. I waited a few days with trepidation, until at last Anne called on Friday to tell me the deal was done and the read through was Monday. The scripts were emailed from Red Productions, but as I had already printed my scenes, I did not have to look at them again. Late on Sunday evening I thought that I might as well have a look in case anything had changed. Everything had changed, the scene had been altered from a Garage to a Pharmacy, and the Soup was now Bath Salts. My blood ran cold as I realised what a Wally I could have been if I had turned up to read the wrong scenario.

Off I went to Media City, really excited, but lurking at the back of my mind was the thought that this was the last chance for them to get rid of me if they thought I was not suitable. Why this paranoia, when in many ways the read through was the only time I would have to meet everybody, and I should just enjoy?

Media City looked magnificent, and the building, which we were using, was called Dock 10. Red Productions had moved in that morning. Everything was beautiful and pristine, what a transformation from Salford Docks where I started work so long ago. We went to a boardroom, where the grandees from Red and ITV, as well as Actors, Director, Writer, people from wardrobe, makeup publicity; this was breath-taking, what was I doing there?

I met the lovely lady who was to play my wife and take a seat next but one to John Simm. We were welcomed by a Red Productions person and the Director Nick Murphy said a few words. Amongst his welcoming remarks something stuck out for me. Nick says, 'You have been cast for your talent and suitability for this show, but most of all because you are nice people'. I had never heard a director say this before, and I really liked it.

We read the first two episodes and took a break. I headed for the loo, and was standing next to John, who asked me how I was. As he had initiated the conversation, I was emboldened and told him that I appeared with him in Cracker. 'Bloody hell, that was seventeen years ago' he said, 'where does the time go?'

I said "Listen mate, I started work aged fifteen on these very Docks, but I'm not telling you how long ago it was, cos if people realise how old I am, they will give this job to someone else".

He said, "don't be daft, tell me". I said, "Fifty six years and two months ago".

The final episode was read, and we dispersed. Although paranoia was still in the back of my mind, it seemed to go well enough and I went home. I had a cup of tea with Helen, and a little nap and waited for further developments.

The 'Shooting Scripts' arrived, and everything seems ok. I wait now for my filming date.

The Call sheet arrived and my scene was to be shot on a Sunday. This makes sense, as the venue was a Chemist shop, which obviously would be open to the public for the rest of the week.

It was now Saturday. We are filming tomorrow in Uppermill near Oldham. Many of my happiest memories are tied up in Oldham, how I met so many people during my spell at the Rep. Barbara Knox, Roy Barraclough, Peter Dudley, Anne Kirkbride. I realised with a jolt that this was over forty years ago, so why was I so consumed with paranoia and fear about the next day? It's only telly; I only had seven lines, what's the problem? The problem was the memory of the unhappy experience from last year with Coronation Street. Let us see what happens in the morning.

Monday now, it is all over; how did it go?

I arrived half an hour early and said hello to Melissa, my 'wife'. We went through the lines a couple of times and then sat in her caravan gossiping, putting the world to rights, and doing the usual actor's thing of bemoaning the fact that we don't get enough work. The rest of the unit return from up on the moors, where they have been examining a gruesome 'body', apparently very realistic and they are cold, summer has gone!

In the chemist shop, two lovely girls who work there normally were looking after us. We ran it once for rehearsal and I am reprimanded for saying 'these' instead of 'this' in my opening line. This was fine, it gave me a jolt and made me concentrate even more. John Simm seemed to be doing nothing at all during the early part of this scene, but just by a twitch of his eyebrows or a flicker of his eyes, he conveyed so much. True genius acting, look and learn.

During the afternoon we ran it six or so times from different camera angles until Nick (Murphy) is satisfied and called that 'a wrap'.

I was elated. I seemed to have 'gotten away with it,' again. The adrenaline started to disperse, and I could now relax. The production has good vibes, the acting talent on show was immense, and the writing was taut. There was no reason whatsoever for it not to be a great piece of work, let's wait and see. As for me, why my paranoia? I do not know. You would think that at my age, I could just relax and enjoy the experience, but I have agonised over seven lines. However, I felt more alive and energised than for months. I am addicted to the whole shebang. I have been doing it for more than fifty years and I love it.

I am going to badminton now, to give these old farts a drubbing.

A month before transmission.

Email from Chris Lunt… 'Jim, your scene was warm and funny, well acted and everyone liked it. Unfortunately, in the greater storyline, the fact that

Farrow (Sim), would not realise that the day was his son's birthday, did not ring true. Reluctantly, your scene has not made the final cut.'

Me, paranoid? Mmmmm…

44: Home Fires

My agent's assistant Anne phoned to ask me to make a self-taped audition, which I hate. She laughed at my lack of computer skills, and sent over the script by email. I took my laptop up to my office and did my best. Obviously, the lighting, sound and so on were terrible quality but I sent it to her anyway.

Two days later, I was in the middle of a badminton game when my phone rang.

"Hello darling" said Elizabeth, "where are you?"

When I told her, she said, "get someone else to play and sit down, I want to talk to you".

I got someone else to take my place and sat down.

She said, "the people we sent the tape to love it, and you've got the job".

That was good news, but what followed was just incredible.

"They want you for a full series. It's a major programme and the money reflects this".

I was in a daze. This sort of thing doesn't happen to me.

Later at home, I had another call from Elizabeth. She wanted to tell me a little of how this job came about. She told me that my wife in the programme was to be Jacqueline Pilton. This made me really happy because not only was she a wonderful actress, but we had worked together on Blackpool (the TV programme) ten years ago, and got on so well. Apparently at the read through, the director came up to Jacky and told her that they couldn't find a 'husband' for her although they had searched everywhere, did she know anyone who might be suitable. Jacky, I found out later, immediately said "what about Jim Whelan, we got on really well in Blackpool".

The important Casting Director said the same, and Jacky mentioned my name again, hence the self-taped audition. They were starting filming in a week's time and had no time left to go through the normal casting process.

I had a call from Christian the second Assistant Director, informing me that I would be needed for rehearsals in London in a couple of days. My

150

tickets were booked by the company, and I turned up at the rehearsal rooms. Jacqueline greeted me, and after a hug, she told me about what had happened at the read through. She said that after the euphoria of getting the job had worn off a little, she began worrying that her 'husband' would turn out not to be compatible. It can be so important in a long running series that you get on, or life can be really miserable for some months. There were no such worries for us, as we get on so well, and are genuinely fond of each other.

The director Bruce, said hello, and told me that they had been scouring the actor's lists trying to find someone for my part. I'm sure he was just being kind and welcoming, but it was good of him. Samantha Bond introduced herself. She was currently in the West End in the musical 'Dirty Rotten Scoundrels'. She was lovely and friendly, and we started rehearsing our scenes. I think I learned more in that hour than in the last ten years. We said cheerio, and I was back on the train within half an hour.

I have scripts for episodes 1-3. I don't even speak in episode one but am a presence in the fictional village of Great Paxford as the gardener and general handyman in the Barden house. Everybody knows me as 'Thumbs'. Jacky is known as 'Cookie'.

A medical is required for a long running role – I presume for insurance purposes – and I am booked in to see a private doctor in St Ann's Square in Manchester. A lovely doctor told me that everything seems OK and I leave her office thinking for the hundredth time what a lucky bugger I am. Having been a sixty a day smoker in my youth (I stopped 50 years ago), and drinking up to a bottle of whisky a day at my worst (I stopped 20 odd years ago), I seem to have escaped any major health issues.

I keep receiving scripts, amendments, shooting schedules, most of which don't affect me. I get a call from the costume department, asking me to go to the location in Cheshire for a fitting. This I am happy to do. The programme title has changed. It is now Home Fires. Perhaps the Jambusters name was a bit flippant? I scour the press release, and my name appears at the very end of a long list of famous people. I don't care, my name is there. My first filming day is still two weeks off, I can't wait.

I visited the unit base in Beeston, and met the lovely Lucy costume designer, who fitted me out with three different costumes, one for best, one for everyday, and one for scruffy gardening type work.

I had a short back and sides from the makeup department. I am all set. I have ten days before my first scene, which is a big set piece wedding. I have no dialogue in this, and just a few dancing shots with Jacky, no pressure at all, can't wait.

First day's filming today. I arrived in good time, setting out from home at 5.45. It never ceases to amaze me how much traffic is around even at that time. Greeted by everybody, I am shown to a very nice trailer, and even receive a card from the production team welcoming me on board. That's a first.

We had a gigantic wedding scene these two days. It couldn't have been better from mine and Jacky's point of view. The Director Bruce was very scrupulous about making sure that Cookie and Thumbs are well featured and receive plenty of close ups. This tells me that he is aware of their place in the village life, and in the household of the Bardens.

At the end of the second day, we have a little nostalgic dance. The Village is saying goodbye to its young men. Cookie and Thumbs finish up sitting next to Mrs Barden (Sam Bond). Although she has been a joy to work with, I am conscious of her standing, and I am trying not to pull focus. After the final rehearsal, she abruptly got up and walked over to the second cameraman whose job it was just to film her close up. I feared the worst, my paranoia never very far away. It seemed she had asked the cameraman to concentrate on us, and to forget about her. Gosh, such generosity is not always evident in our circumstances. I am gobsmacked.

Over the two days, not many of us have dialogue, with it being a wedding, so there is a lot of high spirited banter. Someone spotted that for some reason, Jacky and I had the biggest trailer. This caused 'outrage', especially from Chris Coghill, who said he was getting on to his agent immediately. It seemed that the only reason this happened was because they had run out of smaller vans to hire and if they suddenly gave the big one to any of the principals, they couldn't take it back after the big scenes, and this would be trouble. I said that they would be welcome to call and use my shower.

Home, and comatose after the first two days, but I am well content with proceedings. There is a buzz about the set, a terrific script, and sublime actors. Bruce, who is directing the first three episodes, has a calm assurance about him and while nobody can predict how a series will turn out, we are all so hopeful. My dialogue starts soon, and I am ready.

Dialogue today. Coming up to our scene, Jacky and I are sitting in the pub. People think that at my age, things should be easier but when I am surrounded by Cameramen, Sound Technicians, and Props men, makeup girls powdering my nose, background artistes placed, and Wardrobe girls checking that my tie is straight, my nerves are jangling. We have rehearsed, and a few short notes are given by Bruce. These are really important. He can see things which Jacky and I don't even think about and are unfailingly pertinent to the reactions of the characters.

"Action".

We wait for two regulars to enter the Bar, and comment on them. My words are nearly right, but I say something slightly not according to the script. No-one says anything, and we have to go again for some technical reason. This time all seems well. That's good, and my nerves subside a little. We shoot the scene from several angles, and after two and a half hours, we are done.

My drive back home is a nightmare. The M6 is clogged, and a trip that should take an hour, takes over two. At home, I am trying to stay awake, but am in bed by ten, and asleep by five past.

The next day, I remember the rest of our scene. The camera panned after our dialogue to another table in the bar. Doctor Campbell (Ed Stoppard) is enjoying a drink after his surgery. His wife (Frances Grey) comes in and voices her disquiet at him possibly going to war. She breaks down, and they play the most deliciously tender scene. If this is typical of the quality of acting on show, we could be onto something special.

One of the younger stars says to me later. "You're always so cheerful".

I said nothing, but I felt like telling her that for me, this is 'living the dream'. I am so happy, I could burst!

This is the day after Cookie and Thumbs' main scenes, and I must write this down to put it in to some perspective. I am called to Beeston for 0845 but set off at 6am to beat the traffic. I am the only member of the cast who drives himself to the location, but it is my choice. I arrive at 7 o'clock ish, the caterers have just started serving breakfast and I have a bacon sandwich. It tastes like sawdust, but this is not the cook's fault. I am worried about my dialogue. Having had the script for four weeks and only having five lines, what could go wrong, why am I so apprehensive?

Jacky arrives, and we go through our lines. It is such a comfort to have someone like her alongside. I love her acting, we seem to have a rapport. We are fine.

Makeup, haircut, costume all sorted. Samantha Bond and the delightful young Daisy Badger say hello. We are taken to the location, the heart-stoppingly beautiful Haughton Hall, not at all a forbidding place, but full of character and warmth. It is not a 'museum piece', but a family home, and our resting room contains children's books and other evidence of a well-used house.

The Assistant Director calls us to our set, on the staircase of the main corridor. We run lines to block the scene. Bruce's first note is, "why is everyone whispering?" We don't really know why, but if the first character to speak keeps their voice down, everyone else follows suit. We giggle about this, and go again, Bruce is satisfied (for now), and calls the crew to watch. We run again, and then are told to rest while the camera and lighting are set. All the time, the pressure is building in my mind. We are called back after twenty minutes, and now to business. Run through for the camera to see, some short notes, and on we go.

The scene is shot a couple of times. Bruce is not happy about my delivery. It seems that I am 'too big', I know what he means. When you only have a few lines, they assume gigantic importance to you, this shows in your performance. We do it yet again, and I try to rein myself in. I think I manage that but fail to hit the exact mark for one of my speeches. We go again. This time, someone else stumbles on a line, so we go again. Next time, someone else fails to hit the exact mark, we go again. After a few more takes, Bruce is satisfied. There is no respite for me, because the next set up is for the camera to favour me. This is now the epicentre of my existence. For the next half an hour the camera, makeup, sound, props, director, assistant are all on me. If they knew how I felt, they would be horrified. I can think of nothing else but "please, let me get this right", and I am terrified.

"Action".

Off we go. In retrospect, I would be 60% satisfied with this take, and I think we might have to go again. Bruce says "Good", and on we go to everyone else's close-ups. This goes on for some time, and after nearly three hours, the scene is done.

That last paragraph sounds self-serving and whingeing. If it is such a bloody faff, and causes so much tension and terror, why do it? The answer is I do not know. I have friends who just breeze through this sort of situation, and sometimes I wish that I could. On the other hand, I am me, and that is how I roll. I have mentioned to other better-known actors than me, that I could not do this every day. They said without exception that this fright lessens the longer you do it, so maybe bigger parts are the answer? There is no doubt that to go into long running series like Coronation Street, where everyone seems to have been doing it for years, causes trepidation, and although people are unfailingly kind and helpful, being a 'stranger', is daunting.

Having said all of that, I loved every second of 'Home Fires'. I loved the other actors, I loved turning up on location, and being welcomed. I loved being frightened. I loved the 'buzz'.

We are waiting now for the scripts for episodes 4-5-6, they must arrive soon, the read through is just over a week away. I can't wait.

The scripts arrive for episodes 4&5. I devour them. Thumbs has one line in episode 4, and two in episode 5. My reaction is a mixture of disappointment and relief, but my character is alluded to throughout, and appears in some other scenes so everything is fine. We are emailed to say that the read through is at ITV, London on Tuesday next, at 9am. It seems that episode 6 will not be ready as it is still being worked on.

On the day of filming, I get up at 4.45, am out of the house showered and shaved by 5.15 for the drive to Manchester. I park right next to the Station for the first time ever, so there is something to be said for rising before dawn. I arrive at Euston, and as I have time, walk the mile or so to Grays Inn Road. It is a very impressive building. In reception, is the Director for episodes 4-6, Robert Quinn. He says hello in a lovely soft Irish brogue, and I ascend to the fifth-floor boardroom. I am met by a lovely lady executive, and I am told that they love the rushes of the first block. That is reassuring, and the cast start to arrive. It is a cliché that actors become very close for a short time, but it's absolutely true. I realise as I chat to the others, that we all have the same doubts and fears, and there is a real feeling that we are all going through the same experiences. We greet like long lost relatives and it is schmaltzy, but nice.

The read through is fine. When there is sometimes a small hiatus, for example one of the young actors comes in a little too soon, the senior character said, 'do you mind I haven't finished'. This is lovely banter, and dissolves some of the tension. After all, there are so many senior executives in attendance that some of us (me) are quite intimidated.

We finish, and I share a taxi back to Euston with Jacky, Graeme Hawley (John Stape from Corrie), and a young actress Jodie Hamblett. On the train home, we have a fascinating conversation with Graeme, about his Coronation Street years. The pressure that the soap actors are under to produce two and a half hours of TV a week is immense, and it is to his credit that he remains a normal, happy, down to earth chap.

Script revisions for Episodes 4-5 arrive, and I have another line. This time it's a little joke which Thumbs makes. Writing this, it is so petty to count the lines, but to me it is somehow validation that my character is needed. That is all I want. I am under no illusion that the difficulty they apparently had in casting Thumbs is surely that they could not ask a 'name' to do it because of the lack of dialogue. Then they scoured the lists of small part actors of a certain age (ahem!) and didn't find anyone suitable. By a lucky happenstance, and being friendly with someone (Jacky), from ten years ago, I am here. No complaints from me.

Episode 6 arrives, no lines for Cookie and Thumbs.

Shooting schedule arrives for block 2.

Disaster!

A dark cloud has been hovering over me since day one of this programme. I have told myself it is unlikely to happen. When I agreed to do the television programme, there was a slight possibility that it would impinge upon the dates for a Panto, which I agreed to do last March. I love Panto but I had not done one for the last ten years or so. I did not want to travel and live in Digs at my age over Christmas. Duggie Chapman out of the blue offered the part of Henchman in Snow White, starring Jimmy Cricket. I was happy to accept. Decent money, and 40-minute commute, perfect. The fly in the ointment, and something which was nagging at me, was that the TV finishes shooting on the 5th December, the Panto starts on the 2nd December. I keep telling myself that as my involvement in Home Fires for the final block of three episodes is only five days, the odds are firmly in my favour that none of these would fall in the first week of December.

With the precision of a homing missile, three of the five days fall in the first week of December. These are all big scenes which include nearly the entire cast.

I discuss things at length with Elizabeth. She assures me that this situation is far from unknown, and that she will speak to Duggie, and sort it out. I feel terrible. I have never been in this situation. The Panto casts are mostly sorted in March, presumably so that the actors are tied to the show. This is acceptable, but surely one could not be expected to refuse a TV offer, with more money, and all the ancillaries which can accompany a successful series? I am on tenterhooks waiting for the storm to break.

It is Monday morning, over a month until rehearsals for Snow White start, if indeed I am still involved. I am going to play badminton as a bit of exercise might clear my head. I have had a terrible weekend worrying about the situation. I don't know if Elizabeth has spoken to Duggie, or will the 'explosion' happen today? I keep trying to justify my position to myself, but however I call it, I have agreed to two projects. The fact that anyone might have done the same is scant consolation, let us see what happens.

Elizabeth calls to tell me that Duggie was really nice and agreed to put a 'Deputy' in for the three School performances. This is such a relief. Elizabeth points out that she has a long standing professional relationship with the Duggie Chapman organisation, and that it is part of an Agent's job to look after her clients. I am lucky to be so well represented.

My first day on block two.

No worries for me. A civilised call time and a gentle trundle to Cheshire.

How lovely it is to be greeted by the other actors. We do not often meet 'en masse,' as everybody is in their own little bubble, so we all have some catching up to do. Samantha Bond asks about my house move, I find out about her daughter's stage debut in London, the caterers seem to have changed, but the core crew are all reassuringly familiar.

Robert Quinn is our new director. He says hello, and we briefly exchange pleasantries. He is the first in every day, supervises things all day long, and is the last one to leave. How they keep it up is beyond me. Robert has a keen sense of humour, which pleases me no end.

To the 'Great Paxford' village hall for two interlocking scenes, one for the 'Spencer' character to affirm that he stands by his decision to declare himself a 'Conchie', and the second where all the action takes place during a film show. There are about forty background artists for this scene, mostly from the surrounding area. A newspaper ad went out asking if local people would like to be involved. These people are not your 'hard bitten' extras (of which I was one when I started), but nice, gentle, mostly ladies from the Cheshire villages. We have a somewhat fraught day, but the main characters carry everything off with their usual aplomb, and it all ends well.

During the film watching sequence, Thumbs is placed next to the projection man. This is lovely for me, as I can chat in between takes to the operator who owns it. I learn a lot. I slightly blot my copybook when I am told by Robert, the Director to chat during the take with him. This I do, but apparently, I am moving my hands too much. 'Too many hand gestures Jim', says Robert. I flick a tiny V sign as a joke. "I saw that" he said. Thank goodness he has a sense of humour (I hope!).

Ten days later, we have a gigantic scene in the cellars of Cholmondley Castle cellars. This consists of lots of women and children being shown to the air raid shelter in the Barden house. The whole unit has been moved six miles up the road. I find long long-johns in my trailer, and for the first time, don them thinking that the Castle cellars sound cold. In fact, they are stifling. The heating for the whole building starts there, and within minutes I have to take them off. The actors are all sitting in a dungeon like room deep underground (it seems), and if the public could see our glamorous leading ladies in various stages of scruffiness (hair rollers, fleeces, boots etc.), lots of illusions would be shattered.

It is a hard and laborious day, especially for the background artistes. These are mainly ladies and children as most men would be away at war. The kids with pigtails, ankle socks, and sensible shoes are especially nostalgic to me. I am by some distance the oldest main cast member and sometimes I feel it.

Despite the long day, there are lots of delightful moments for me. Chatting to Ed Stoppard, Sam Bond, and the others is an absolute joy. I don't want it ever to end.

Back again. This time I am three days into Panto rehearsal, and it necessitated a day away from that, not ideal. The powers that be, however, quite understand and recognise that this TV job must take precedence. I meet my 'Deputy', Chris, who has been drafted in to fill in for my two missing performances. He played the part two years ago for Duggie Chapman, and is au fait with the script, this is a relief, and Chris is off to start his own Panto (which is a shorter run than Preston) in Barrow.

I have no dialogue today, but I am privileged to be part of a lovely, gentle, poignant scene between the two sisters (Sam Bond and Ruth Gemmel), where they worry out loud about the safety of Ruth's Vicar husband who is away at the front. I marvel at how the two ladies extract so much pathos and gentle concern from the scene with the minimum of movement and gestures. This is rare understated acting and is a joy to watch.

Last two days now. Setting off at dawn, having to scrape frost from the car is so different from when we started in September and had two months of glorious sunshine. We are back at the beautiful Haughton Hall.

I have had a traumatic opening to our Panto. We opened in a 10.15 am show and played to about two hundred and fifty primary school children. They were lovely, but one of our self appointed Directors, (Duggie's wife) castigated me in front of the whole company, mainly because some Velcro failed and the leg of my breeches was falling down, and because I wasn't up to speed on a song with tricky words and movement. Both things are correct. My excuse if I have one, is that six working days of rehearsal is not enough for me, and there was never a music call to reinforce the song. I am mortified and have a miserable afternoon. The lovely Kristina (Snow White) rehearses me in the song and the company manager (also wardrobe it seems) mends my breeches. The evening show is a full house and the Press night is a triumph, and feeling a bit better, I take my two days away and decamp to Home Fires.

My final day is once again a gigantic scene at Haughton Hall, where the Great Paxford villagers are herded into the shelters for the first air raid of the war. We had been warned that a film crew from our local Granada region and stills photographers would be in attendance. Jacky and I are grabbed, and we gabble a few lines which are shown on the Granada news programme that evening. The scene goes well, and my involvement is over. The first Assistant Director shouts out the names of the ten characters who are finished, and Samantha Bond gives me a lovely hug, I can't help a tiny tear escaping.

This has been one of the best experiences of my life. Although my involvement has been small, I have worked on what could be a great drama and have spent all my time on Home Fires with Samantha Bond. For an old fogey, heading swiftly to my dotage, how could anyone have foreseen this? We will not know for months whether our show is any good, or if the public will watch, but I will never forget it.

45: Moving Home

Helen and I had given long and careful thought and had decided to move.

Lucy and Joe had returned from five years working in Kuala Lumpur, trailing their delightful little red-haired character with them. He is Thomas and he seems to love eating, singing, and dancing in equal measure. They have settled in Eastbourne, bought a house, and found jobs, so this is where they will stay for the foreseeable future.

Andrew and Ruth were still in Henfield. Andrew was working for a year in Chichester Hospital and looking for Consultant Anaesthetist jobs. Ben and Lucas were growing fast, and we found that the long drive from Bury was more taxing than ever, especially with the extra bit to Eastbourne. Thinking of moving was so daunting, having lived in West Drive (in three different houses) since the day we got married just short of forty years ago.

Our friends, Helen's walking mates, the church where she does flowers, my badminton three times a week and friends network built over four decades were discussed, but our wanting to be near to our children and grandchildren was our main wish and we started looking for Estate Agents.

We decided upon one after seeing three, and the sign went up. Within a week we had two visits from large extended families, which resulted in derisory offers. These we dismissed out of hand, not being desperate to take any offer and we settled down for what could be a long wait.

As luck would have it, I got the Home Fires job. This was much more convenient from Bury, and I also had the panto in Preston to do, so it was better that we didn't move before the New Year. Nothing happened anyway, so we just got on with things.

I finished Home Fires and went straight into panto in Preston. A couple came to view the house and said that they were really interested. We had heard it all before, but sure enough they made an acceptable offer, so we were on!

Off to Eastbourne to look at houses. Now that we had sold, things were more urgent, but looking in our price bracket was very depressing. We realised that there was a disparity in price, but with one exception, everything seemed cramped and poor value. The exception was a four-bedroom terrace in Longland Road, Old Town. The drawback was that we would have to do a lot of work decorating wise, and it was almost out of our bracket. Fortunately, the Home Fires money was an unexpected bonus, so we made an offer, and after some bargaining, it was accepted.

Moving day arrived, tempers became frayed. I love to get rid of things, Helen hoards. I seemed to spend forever packing boxes in the garage and paid numerous visits to the tip, a removal firm was booked.

We have hit a possible snag. The people buying our house want to move in quite quickly, but our new house could not be vacated in time, and there was a month's time difference. We could have played hardball, but I was convinced that if anything went wrong with our sale, the whole pack of cards could have collapsed, and we might have lost Longland Road. We decided to vacate early to accommodate the purchasers, stored our furniture, and spent a month homeless.

Fortunately, our friends without exception came to our rescue. We spent ten days with Barbara and David in Bury, moved to Ali and Rod in Wem in Shropshire, and spent two weeks with Tony and Jean in Linton, Cambridgeshire. It was very disorientating to be on the road with no home, but it brought home to us the value of good friends.

We arrived in Eastbourne, stayed with Lucy and Joe, and picked up the key. Entering the house and looking around was profoundly depressing. The paintwork all over was a muddy dark maroon sort of colour. There was a room, which was completely purple, and one that was orange. The carpets were mostly shot. What a mess. It was hard to hide our dismay, but Lucy bless her, pointed out the advantages, such as the 'en suite' in the attic, the giant conservatory, and the lovely location. She told us about a decorator who did some work for them, and he came to visit. Steve was his name, and he was a nice man. He looked all around for an hour, said that he had never seen anything like it, and gave us an estimate. He would have to come every day for a month and give three coats to cover. He was waiting for a job on a school, but they were having too many meetings etc, and his patience was exhausted with them, so he could start right away. We agreed, and he started.

Although Steve was a lovely man, him arriving every day before eight meant that we felt most uncomfortable. He worked extremely hard, but we had to keep moving to different rooms to accommodate him and suddenly a month seemed an awfully long time. Eventually we saw the light at the end of the tunnel and a fine house was emerging. The main transformation was when the carpets were fitted. Steve finished on the Tuesday, and Bill the carpet man, and two others arrived on the Wednesday. Hall stairs and landings (2), two bedrooms, and flooring for the attic bathroom were all fitted in one day. Meanwhile, I had my little garden shed, which caused much hilarity, and we could start putting up pictures. Finally, we were home.

Andrew and Ruth delivered a bombshell; he had accepted a job as a Consultant Anaesthetist in Invercargill, New Zealand. We knew that he was considering a move abroad but hoped for somewhere not so far away. However, it was a terrific job and a great opportunity for an adventure as a family. Lucas hadn't started school; Ben was at an age when moving wouldn't be too great a disruption. This is possibly their last chance before Andrew is tied to a Consultant post, so they go for it.

The ramifications for them of letting their house in Henfield, clearing the debris from ten years, and the red tape hoops to jump through were daunting, but after three months, the moment arrived. They stayed with us for a few days, and with their furniture in a giant container going by sea, they disappeared from Eastbourne in a people carrier. It was a surprisingly banal morning. The boys were more excited about the airplane than thinking that they might not see us old fogies for a while, but that's the way it should be, and we were happy for their great adventure. Of course, we missed them, but it is not about us, they are off to see the world. Who could blame them?

When they had gone, Helen and I disappeared to different parts of the house. I think that she was having a quiet weep upstairs. I went into the garden and did a little pottering. I tried not to think about it, but my heart did hurt. The little boy who used to fling himself at me had left with his own children. I knew it was not about us, but my goodness they left a massive hole. God speed.

46: Snatch

Elizabeth rang, another self-taped audition. Peculiar one, because it was for a cockney little old tailor in a gangster series based on the Guy Ritchie movie.

I read the script and went upstairs to my 'office'. You would think I would be a dab hand at this by now, but I'm not. I find it excruciating but dressed up with a tape measure round my shoulders. I did it six times and emailed it to my Agent. For a few days you get a little bit of hope, but then after a week, you know it's gone.

Three weeks later Elizabeth called and said, "I bet you'd forgotten about 'Snatch', but they like you, you've got the job, guess where it's filming, yes Manchester."

Well fancy that! A week later, I was on the train and when I turned up at Piccadilly station, a car was waiting to take me to the Unit Base. We were based at the old Granada studios which had been so much a part of my life, and I went for a wardrobe fitting and makeup check. The hollowed-out shell of the building, and the wreck of the Coronation Street set were so sad to look at, but I suppose things had to move on.

I was in the shower at 5.30 the next day, I was picked up from the hotel at six. I met my co star for today, a fascinating young man called Michael Obiora, playing 'Naz' in several episodes. I mentioned to him that I first appeared at these studios some fifty-five years ago. Thinking I would not bore him with anything else, I shut up, but he insisted that I tell him all about it. What seemed to fascinate him most was the early Coronation St studio shoots which had to be done in one twelve-minute take. This would have been half of one episode and I suppose editing was difficult in those days, but the pressure as the minutes ticked on was immense. If an actor 'dried', or a serious mistake like a camera appearing in shot, then we would have to go back to the beginning. There were four giant TV cameras, very carefully choreographed for maybe ten scenes, and it was amazing to see how things worked; everybody knowing exactly what do do, everything in its place. The sigh of relief was palpable when the twelve minutes ended with the Director saying from the gallery. "That's fine studio, on we go.".

The set was an old-fashioned tailor's shop beside Albert Square. The scenes went well enough and we were finished by lunch.

I set off for home.

It had been a lovely and quite unexpected job; I was just glad to be working. Manchester looked smashing, I miss lots of aspects, but the grandson is in Eastbourne and that is the main thing.

I embark on the return journey with some trepidation. Southern Rail were carrying on their disgraceful 'hostage taking' of the commuters on the Victoria to Eastbourne (and everywhere else south of London) line. The trip from Victoria necessitated a diversion via Brighton, arriving in Eastbourne more than an hour later than I should have, but I was simply happy to be home.

47: Series 2, Home Fires

Home Fires first series started transmission on the 3rd of May 2015. Originally, the plan was to show the programme in March, but on the BBC, Poldark was proving a massive hit, and it would have been folly to oppose it. I had seen the episode in Bunbury at the special showing for the northern-based actors, crew, and the local people.

The day after transmission, we found the reviews were a bit sniffy. Several critics seemed to be quite dismissive of the fact that the main – in fact only action – was set completely in a small village. They seemed to be missing the point. That was the intention all along, to show that the womenfolk who were seeing their sons and husbands go off to fight – maybe never to return – were suffering just as much as anyone.

Encouraging signs came from the social media sites, which were almost completely behind the premise that you did not need explosions and close-up carnage to tell a war story. When the viewing figures were published, we were delighted to see that in excess of five million had tuned in. As the series continued, the figures increased to over six million.

From a personal point of view, I was disappointed. The two main scenes with Cookie and Thumbs had been cut due to time constraints. Each episode being only forty-six minutes, due to adverts. This left almost nothing to establish Thumbs in the Barden household, and I feared that I would not survive if there were to be a second series. Nonetheless, I had an intense pride at even being involved, I felt that the acting all round was superb, and it was a programme of which I was so proud.

As the run ended, it was announced that ITV had given the go ahead for a second series. Nothing to do now but wait and hope.

I was with little Thomas in our local park in Eastbourne when Elizabeth rang and said "Darling this is the news you've been waiting for. James Bain has just rung from ITV to book you for the second series".

I was happy, happy, happy. There was nothing to do now but wait for the scripts to see what my involvement would be.

Ten days to read-through, but still no scripts. Things were hotting up. I received calls daily from Wardrobe, makeup, and production people. I was off to Morris Angel's costumiers in London for fittings, and the read through was a week later. On the day of the Read, I also had to go to Harley Street for another medical for insurance purposes.

My scripts arrived for episodes 1, 2 and 3. Thumbs involvement was as before, with Cookie and Thumbs a constant presence in the Barden household. This was really encouraging. It would of course be lovely to have more to do, but this was a major drama with many more important characters, and lots of new storylines, so I was content.

Off to the read-through, it was strange to be approaching London from the south, and I didn't at all like being caught up in the seething mass that was the Victoria line Tube during the morning rush hour.

The cast greeted each other like long lost cousins, and we settled down to read the episodes. There were a lot of changes to the storylines, and some unexplained directorial and staff alterations. Ours as actors was not to reason why, and the scripts were read. They are moving and heartfelt and I think the writers have done a magnificent job. I looked forward to trying to do them justice.

In the afternoon, lots of the cast trooped over to Harley St for medicals, I was once again given a clean bill, always a relief, and waited for the call to start filming.

The first day of filming came. I arrived last night in Chester and booked into the hotel. On the train, I met the lovely Ruth Gemmell, and chatted about everything under the sun. After checking in, I received a text saying that people were meeting in the bar for a drink. I spent a lovely couple of hours chewing the fat with Samantha, Francesca, Ruth, Daisy and Mike (what a name dropper)

An early call, and I was off to the beautiful Haughton Hall. Nice little scene with some dialogue (not a lot) for me, no pressure, lovely!

The following day, another nice little scene with dialogue (one line) for Thumbs. We wrapped early, and I shared a train back to London with Ruth. It is really strange to be heading south to get home, and I arrived in Eastbourne at 11 ish, and got a cab home.

The following week for my next scene. This is a big one for the production, a makeshift camp filled with Czech soldiers. I had no idea that this was so authentic, but it is true that many arrived in Cheshire early in the war.

This is a difficult group of scenes to film. The weather doesn't help as the rain is constant and it is very cold. After being given an early call, I am informed that our one scene, which should have been filmed at 10 am, is changed to the end of the day. This couldn't be worse news for those involved (five of us), and we sit in our vans all day until taken to the location at 5.30pm. The scene involves a crane shot, and everyone is desperate to get it done, presumably the crane is madly expensive.

We manage to get the establishing shots done and break for the day. We are back the following day for the close ups. Because the earlier shots were done in the late afternoon, the close ups also have to wait until then, for 'light continuity'. This means another day waiting and starting at 5pm. We get the scenes done and scramble for the transport to Crewe for the 8pm London express. I finally arrive home at 12.45 a.m. Well knackered but content. I just have to say, that I feel desperately sorry for the background artistes, who have been out in the (mostly) rain for two days. They are good natured and patient, but due to the nature of the job, they have to just wait and suffer.

The read-through for Episodes 4-6 is scheduled for early October but is cancelled because they are still working on the scripts. I do not know how these things work, but presumably they did not meet with expectations, and are rejected. I email Elizabeth with the news, and she replies that she has never known a read-through be cancelled.

Back to Cheshire for my final shoot in block 1, the first three episodes have been a joy. Because I am now staying in the hotel with the cast in Chester, I got to know everyone a lot better. Without doubt, it is lovely. Ed Stoppard makes me laugh so much, so does Leanne Best, with tales of her Scouse Nana. I discuss football with Mike Noble, who is an avid Liverpool fan, as are three of the drivers, and continued to marvel at the Acting talent on view.

First night in the hotel, and episodes 5/6 arrive. I scan these immediately and am consumed with disappointment. There is no sign of Cookie and Thumbs, it looks grim. I am not the only one to feel this way, more important players than me are somewhat sidelined, such is this business.

We finish up the scenes, which are in the Air raid shelters, with 'Bombs' dropping, and lots of mayhem ensuing. Chris Coghill had a lovely speech where he declaims that all the villagers should prepare themselves for invasion, and that the Nazis are merciless. He does this so well, time after time, and I realise yet again that beneath his jokey, blokey exterior, there is a fine actor.

An email from Elizabeth tells me that I am booked for episode 6, so that is a relief, but when I read it there are no lines, and only a tiny appearance. Oh well.

Back home to Eastbourne. I am not needed now for six weeks, so time to relax and play Grandad.

The week of my final appearance on Home Fires started with a change of schedule. We are to film my scenes a day later, no problem for me, so I set off to Chester. As I check in the lovely young scouse girl on reception says to me, "Oh Mr Whelan, I have a message for you, here it is."

It's from Sam:

'Darling Jim, so happy to have you back with us, we are all meeting in the bar at seven, love it if you could join us. '

You have to imagine that said in a thick Liverpool accent to see why it tickled me so much. I did meet everybody and had a smashing night. I met Philip Lowrie, who was Denis Tanner in the first episode of Corrie fifty-four years ago to the day, wow! We had a friend in common, Barbara Knox (Rita in Corrie), and chatted about the old days. He reminded me that for the first few episodes, Corrie went out Live to up to twenty million viewers. How times have changed.

Drastically early 6am call, but as usual nothing went according to plan. It was pouring down and as our scene was outdoors, we are banished to our vans to wait. The weather improves, but by now the hours have run out on the young boy who is integral to the scene, and it's back to the hotel for another night.

A pleasant evening, a gentle drink with the cast, and I realise this may well be my last ever episode and try to remember it.

The next morning, everything went like clockwork, the scene was shot, and by 10 am, we were on the way to Crewe for the London Train.

The little boy Oliver makes me laugh when I first meet him. "Hello, are you playing Noah," I say.

"Yes, who are you?"

"I'm Thumbs." '

"Well, I'm gonna call you fingers."

The long wait for transmission now. How much of Thumbs will remain after the edit? Will it be successful again? Will another series be commissioned, and if so will Thumbs survive? If not, it has been a great experience.

At the risk of being called sycophantic, a little word about Samantha Bond (Mrs B, to me). Without doubt she was the kingpin of this show. She was in more scenes than anyone and was the most important actor. She would never dream of saying this, but I can.

She adopted the 'Head Girl' persona when we were off set, and organized our evenings out in local hostelries, even dividing the bill with scrupulous fairness at the end. I feel guilty, but because I don't drink, she made sure that I pay less. We had great fun off set, and this was due to her. A production reflects its principals, and this was important to the happiness of the shoot.

On set, she is professional and committed. She will help and assist anyone but is ruthlessly critical of herself. The pressure daily, to produce the goods must be immense, but it never spills over into down time. We can have a lovely inconsequential chat about my house move, her children's acting career, my upcoming visit to New Zealand, and so on, then instantly change into 'business' mode when needed. I count myself so fortunate to be working with her.

Three weeks to transmission and I have been approached by local radio and newspapers here in Eastbourne to do some publicity. This is quite fun, and I have no objection. I had better make sure it's OK with ITV publicity department.

48: Why Was Home Fires Cancelled?

Series Two aired to some acclaim. The viewing figures were extraordinary and social media loved it. Main cast members were interviewed on national TV, and it seemed that the love for the characters and stories was constant.

Three weeks after the final episode, came a bald email saying that Home Fires would not be re-commissioned.

The ITV statement said, 'We are tremendously proud of what Home Fires has achieved, but we are refreshing our portfolio.'

Outrage followed from fans of the show, and a young lady named Kerryn Groves set up a petition. Within two weeks, over twenty-six thousand people had signed it, and Kerryn printed out the signatures and was driven by her dad to London, to present the petition. Kerryn, who uses a wheelchair, was refused admission to the ITV building on the South Bank and gave the six hundred and sixty pages to the mail receiving point. The following day, she received a letter from Kevin Lygo's office apologising, and saying that they had received the petition.

A website sprang up. There were articles in National Newspapers and people like Julie Summers, author of Jambusters – the book on which Home Fires is based – and Kerryn, were interviewed on several Radio programmes. I had been offered an appearance on BBC Radio Sussex, ostensibly to talk about 'interesting' people who have moved to Sussex. I agreed and had a lovely fifteen-minute rant about Home Fires to the bemusement of the Producer. During all this furore, there was silence from ITV.

A young lady, Jessica Taylor, had started a Facebook page with lots of information. It seemed that the fans are settling in for a long battle. A Home Fires campaign song had been written and released by Geraldine Pointing, and a save the Home Fires official group, was now well established.

Four years after the cancellation, the campaign showed no signs of abating. The petition stood at fifty-six thousand signatories, and there were questions which ITV needed to answer.

1) Why cancel a programme with over six million viewers?

2) Is it not deeply insulting to your audience to leave a story with all the strands left in the air?

3) What incentive has anyone to watch any ITV Drama, when it can be summarily axed leaving the time they have expended buying in to the stories completely wasted?

4) Does it not mean anything to you that it was watched in one hundred and thirty-five countries and territories, mostly to great acclaim?

5) Strong female-led dramas are rare, why axe one that is so well loved.

There were many more additional questions to be answered. Could ITV just keep their silence and further insult their audience by pretending they do not exist? Yes, I know it's only a TV programme, but how can such an injustice be allowed to go unchallenged?

I know that some may see this article as the ramblings of a 'washed up' actor, but I have received emails from America, Australia, Canada, New Zealand, South Africa, to name only a few.

After so long in this business, I have no fear of the 'Powers that be'.

My race is just about run. I shall spend my remaining days playing with my grandboys.

49: Wild Bill

Call from Elizabeth to go to London to Sarah Crowe Casting. Small part in one episode of a six-part TV series starring American superstar Rob Lowe.

Had a good train journey and found my way to a business style complex in North London.

I had one line to chew over, was greeted warmly by Xanthe, Sarah's assistant and did my line 4 different ways. She asked me on camera to say a little about myself. I told her that I would recount some of the material from the talks which I do down here on the South Coast and said, 'just wave when you've had enough'. She let me continue for about 5 minutes and I left the office quite pleased. I thought that I had done all that I could and now it's down to the imponderables, do you look like the father of the policeman they want you for? Are you the right age? Do they like you? etc.

A few days later, I had got the job. Wow, four scenes, two with Rob Lowe, what a Christmas present.

The usual mayhem when you get the part had commenced.

Emails containing the script, four more lines. Calls from makeup asking if I could start growing a 'tache, call from the production office to arrange a costume fitting and a call from 1st AD Chris, welcoming me. Call from Elizabeth firming up the dates, next week. This was short notice, but I prefer that. We fixed the costume fitting for the day before my first shooting day and I will stay over for an early start.

On the train for my costume fitting and makeup check, I had a call from Chris to let me know that my driver would be waiting at Victoria. Whisked to the location and spent a happy couple of hours being fussed over and cosseted by people dressing me and making my moustache more luxuriant. Said hello to Anthony Flanagan, who is the son whose dad I am playing. He seems a bit surprised that I think my character has early onset dementia, but I was told this and my performance reflects it.

After an early night, I was picked up at 6 am and after visiting Wardrobe and Makeup, was taken to a Working Men's Club. I was in my element here being a bingo caller, I spent thirty odd years in clubs like this playing second fiddle to bingo, so I knew it well. When I said hello to the Director, John Hardwick, I mentioned my dementia, but it seems that this is no longer the case. I am given half a dozen more lines, all 'bingo' numbers with which I am familiar. We started shooting. It's a bit tricky in that the meat of the scene is an exchange between Rob Lowe and Angela Lonsdale and the bingo bloke needed to carefully orchestrate his numbers in between the dialogue so as not to obscure their lines. This is fine, lets me get acclimatised and I can say that I have played a scene with a Hollywood superstar, although we do not meet, have no dialogue and no eye contact of any sort.

I am 'handed over' to the second camera team to film some close-ups. This is lovely, the second camera Director is a delightful girl named Claire Tailyour. She directs me with skill, compassion and panache, getting some nice close-up shots.

I had the weekend off and returned on Monday lunchtime for some night shoots on a disused council estate. My main scenes were with my 'son', who was attaching a security chain to my door; my character lived alone and was in danger from a man who is apparently murdering pensioners. Working with Anthony was a delight, he was effortlessly professional and we got on well. Once again Claire took over for my close-up shots. This was a rare luxury for a small part player, and I was grateful. How much of my close work would survive the editing process was anybody's guess?

In a later scene, I had a brief exchange with Rob Lowe, a line to him, to which he had to respond; we shot the scene and it was the only connection I had with him. He seemed quite ruthlessly professional and was whisked away as soon as our scene ended. Having said that, I had noticed him making conversation with some of the background artistes who were in the bingo hall the previous day. This was always a good sign; our worlds could not be further apart, and I was a little in awe of the Hollywood star.

We finished at 10.30 and I was given the choice of staying in London or catching the midnight train home. I opted for the train as I had something to do in Eastbourne the next day. I arrived home at 2.30 am, shattered but happy, I felt as if I acquitted myself as well as I could, great job, really pleased with it.

50: Eastbourne

Helen and I are so pleased to be down here in Eastbourne. The weather is better, we are within a couple of miles of Beachy Head, and the surroundings could not be further removed from post war Salford. There is a view of the sea from our bedrooms, and we are gently settling in. It is lovely to have Lucy, Joe and especially little Thomas nearby. We take him to school and pick him up once a week, and he runs us ragged. I am busily helping him to save the Universe from certain baddies, but when I complain about my status as his assistant, he treats me with the disdain I deserve.

Lucy and Joe are both teaching in Eastbourne. They are conscientious and Joe has become Head of English and assistant Head, at his school. We love to attend Lucy's school plays. She is adored by her pupils, and quite rightly so!

We desperately miss Andrew, Ruth, Ben and Lucas, and we are grateful to see them every week on Facetime. We travelled to Invercargill in New Zealand to see them all in January 2016. They seem happy and having spent fourteen years in the NHS, I am sure Andrew is appreciating the less pressurised environment. I can still scarcely conceive that my little mate is now a Hospital Consultant. Ruth works at the same Hospital as an Occupational Therapist, the boys are growing fast, Ben's next Birthday will see him a Teenager. How did that happen?

51: Speaker

I was asked to give a talk at a local U3A about my fifty years as an actor. I enjoyed it so much, that I rehearsed an hour's worth of stuff and started doing it to the Women's Institute, Probus and various other groups. They have proved popular and an enjoyable experience. No actor needs too much encouragement to show off, and I am no exception.

In my opening remarks, I tell them "if you ask an old ham to come and talk about himself, you have only yourself to blame".

The differences between my talks and the gladiatorial experiences of Working Men's Clubs from so many years ago, could not be starker. Here, people have come to see you, are unfailingly polite and attentive and often I receive an email following my appearance thanking me. I loved the Working Men's Clubs, but at my age, prefer the talks.

A fellow Speaker advised me that I would suit Cruise ships, so I applied to Cunard/P&O and was given an audition. This took place at their headquarters in Southampton with the heads of all the different departments from the various Ships in attendance. Despite some nerves, I called upon my long years of experience, and acquitted myself well enough.

I was accepted and my first cruise was booked for May 2020. Helen, of course, would come with me, we would pay her air fare, but this would be more than made up with, by the expenses they would pay me.

I rehearsed four talks with PowerPoint presentations which P&O required. I think that this added to the interest because I could show clips which had never been seen before, having found them online. I also have many photographs from up to fifty years ago.

Unfortunately, Covid 19 put paid to this, and of course to all of my talks. I am hoping to resume soon, but I have some doubts about cruising. It could be some time.

52: Conclusions

There is no way that I want this tale to come across as a 'hard luck' story, or a misery

Reading back through some parts, it makes me sound like a bit of an unhappy person. Nothing could be further from the truth. I am very blessed, and when I weigh up the balance, I am well out in front.

Unhappily, my older brother Chris died a little time ago. He is sadly missed, but he had had a fine career locally in Salford especially, playing the piano and singing in pubs and clubs for many years.

My younger brother Phil died also, leaving a tremendous void. He left a daughter and three lovely girls, grandchildren whom he absolutely adored. The turn out and the love expressed from so many at his funeral, spoke volumes of how fond people were of him.

At the time of writing, I am as fit as a butcher's dog. I have no health problems and will keep on acting until I can physically no longer do it. I will never be a star, and I do not lie awake at nights thinking about it.

On my side of the family, although we don't live in each other's pockets, we are reasonably friendly and in touch, mainly thanks to my sister Eileen. As the only girl, she has inherited the mantle of our mum. She cannot stop working in her own home, tidying and cleaning like a dervish and, as well as looking after her family, she has nursed several friends and relatives, through terminal conditions. She spent the bulk of her working life as a nurse at the Prestwich Hospital, near Bury, and is due enormous gratitude from the rest of us.

My youngest brother Billy has at last found his true vocation as a grandfather. He has a motley crew surrounding him at all times. He and Trish are adored by them, and quite rightly.

I play badminton at the local leisure centre three times a week. We are a group of perhaps forty or so people over fifty years of age and some of the grizzled players have been of an extremely high standard. They take no prisoners, and as I am not of the 'premier league' as they like to call themselves, they put me in my place day after day. They won't even let me swear as they say, "it's not seemly for a vicar."

I was walking down Deansgate in Manchester one day, and a young man I had never seen before stopped me and said, "Are you Jim Whelan?"

I said I was, and he said, "I work in the dubbing department at Granada, we've been putting some music over the funeral scene for Vera Duckworth, and I'm sick of looking at your face." He smiled and walked off. Now that is not something that happens every day.

These little observations from people who think that they know you tickle me. One day whilst waiting nervously to be interviewed at Granada the receptionist looked at me over her half moon glasses and said, "Jim, you look like every vicar or priest I have ever known." Now, was this a testament to my magnificent portrayal of the Corrie 'man of the cloth'? I rather think not, I must just look priestly to folk. When people ask me why I keep getting cast 'in vestments', I reply, "Because I've led a blameless life."

During the many quiet periods, when I cannot get myself arrested, never mind get a part, and people say that they haven't seen me on the 'box' for a while, I like to tell them that I am moribund. This keeps them quiet and gives me time to make a quick exit.

It seems sometimes, that I am on the 'crest of a slump', but the thing is not to become bitter. You also must be careful what you wish for. Suppose I had become the Unigate milkman? Perhaps I might never have met Helen? Perhaps there would be no Andrew, or Lucy, or Ben and Lucas or Thomas? That is something I could never envisage.

I do not often think of my dad, because he meant so little to me, but when I do, I wonder if his selfishness and indifference to us was a result of his own upbringing.

Helen met my mum when she was in hospital with the cancer that eventually killed her. I was glad, and I am always grateful for the hard work and love, which she gave us when we were small. She was an unsophisticated woman and did her best with the pretty miserable hand she was dealt. When we went to see her to tell her that Helen and I were getting engaged she said to me through a few tears, "Jimmy, you must never raise your hand to her." I feel guilty to this day, that because of me and my brothers, she never seemed to have a minute's rest.

Although I do not look back with too many regrets, I do sometimes wonder what sort of a life would have unfolded for me if things were different in my early years. There is no doubt whatsoever in my mind, that if I had ever had a 'proper' job, or career, say as a teacher, or journalist, I would not be an actor.

On the other hand, I would not swap the highs, which I have experienced for a gold clock. The people I have met, the excitement, the adrenaline rush, the sheer joy I feel when I am involved in rehearsing something, is a privilege which I could never replace.

There have been times when this capricious business has driven me to tears of frustration or rage, and there have been times when I have been humiliated in auditions or interviews by insensitive, unfeeling clots.

But whenever I am near to despair….

I have a picture imprinted on my brain of a little lady, sitting in front of the fire sewing buttons on to gentlemen's trousers for 1/6 d a pair.

Thanks for reading!
Jim Whelan